Festive Shapes and Sugar Sprinkles Unleashed

Festive Shapes and Sugar Sprinkles: Cookie Decorating Extravaganza

Sarah Thompson

Table of Contents

INTRODUCTION

Welcome to the enchanting world of "Festive Shapes and Sugar Sprinkles Unleashed: Cookie Decorating Extravaganza," where the art of cookie decoration transforms into a delightful and magical experience. In this e-book, we journeyed through the whimsical universe of festive cookie decorating, exploring the possibilities of combining positive shapes and sugar sprinkles.

The holiday season is a time of joy, celebration, and indulgence in sweet treats. What better way to spread the festive cheer than by creating beautifully adorned cookies that tantalize the taste buds and captivate the eyes? "Festive Shapes and Sugar Sprinkles Unleashed" is your go-to guide for unlocking the secrets of cookie decorating, offering a comprehensive and accessible resource for beginners and seasoned bakers.
As you delve into the pages of this e-book, you'll discover the essential tools and ingredients needed for successful cookie decorating, laying the foundation for your creative endeavors. From mastering basic shapes to exploring intricate designs, each chapter is crafted to guide you through the step-by-step process of creating edible works of art. Unleash your creativity and learn to navigate the world of sugar sprinkles, discovering the myriad ways to use them to elevate your cookie designs.

Whether you're a novice looking to build confidence or an experienced decorator seeking new challenges, "Festive Shapes and Sugar Sprinkles Unleashed" caters to all skill levels. With chapters dedicated to holiday-themed creations, party planning, and even troubleshooting common mistakes, this e-book is designed to be your companion on every step of your cookie-decorating journey.

Get ready to immerse yourself in the joy of festive shapes and the sparkle of sugar sprinkles. Let the "Cookie Decorating Extravaganza" begin, and may your creations be as delightful as the holiday season itself.

CHAPTER I

Essential Tools and Ingredients

List of Necessary Baking Tools

Many enjoy baking, which turns uncooked components into delicious sweets. The correct equipment may make all the difference regarding baking, regardless of your experience level. In addition to facilitating the process, a well-equipped kitchen guarantees that the finished result is a work of art. This post will thoroughly inventory essential baking supplies that any home baker needs to have on hand.

A trustworthy set of measuring equipment is the foundation of each baker's toolset. Baking requires exact measurements because even a tiny variance might affect the result. Accurate portioning of ingredients with a set of measuring cups and spoons guarantees the ideal harmony of flavors and textures in your recipes. Investing in a kitchen scale also adds a degree of accuracy, especially when working with goods like flour, where accuracy is crucial.

Baking is made possible by mixing bowls, an unsung kitchen hero. These bowls are made from various materials, including plastic, glass, and stainless steel, and they are available in multiple sizes to suit a variety of recipes. They can also be used as dough-proofing vessels due to their adaptability. They act as a canvas for mixing and blending components. An assortment of mixing bowls is an essential part of any baker's toolkit, as each has a distinct function in baking.

A solid set of bakeware is essential to the flourishing of baking as an art. Essential bakeware that works with various recipes includes muffin tins, cake pans, and baking sheets. Bakers may get consistent results every time they bake because the robust design and non-stick surfaces guarantee even baking and easy release. The latest innovation in baking, silpat mats provide an eco-friendly substitute for parchment paper and a non-stick surface for handling dough.

The accuracy and control of high-quality measuring tools are essential to any baking project. A trustworthy oven thermometer guarantees a precise oven temperature for baking foods with the right texture and flavor. Similarly, a candy thermometer is handy for tasks requiring exact temperature control, including tempering chocolate or creating caramel. Because the temperature is a controlled variable, this equipment gives bakers the confidence to experiment with various recipes.

Without a reliable and effective mixer, no baker's toolkit is complete. Stand mixers save time and effort by streamlining the mixing and kneading process with solid motors and adaptable accessories. Hand mixers provide a more portable option for bakers who like a more hands-on approach or those with limited kitchen space. The number of baking projects one undertakes, and personal tastes determine which option is best.

The importance of a rolling pin in baked products cannot be emphasized. A sturdy rolling pin is an indispensable tool in the kitchen, used for everything from smoothing out cookie dough to creating the ideal pie crust. Rolling pins made of wood, marble, or silicone each have unique benefits that suit various tastes and baking requirements. Additionally, rolling pins give the baker a physical link with the dough, enabling a hands-on method of shaping and molding different treats.

Pastry brushes have soft bristles and are used for various purposes in baking. These multipurpose tools refine the finished presentation of baked goods, whether used for brushing on melted butter for a golden finish, glazing pastries with egg wash, or adding a sugar syrup to improve shine. A more recent kind that is durable and easily cleaned is silicone brushes. Pastry brushes are evidence of the meticulous attention to detail that turns baking into a creative endeavor.

Precision in the complex realm of baking goes beyond measures to include the fine art of decorating. Piping bags and tips are essential for bakers to infuse their creations with flare and originality. These tools enable bakers to convey their creative vision, from delicate pastry fillings to elaborate cake designs. An ordinary cupcake can become a work of edible art thanks to the many different available tips.

A range of cooling racks is essential to any baker's toolkit. These basic but essential tools help baked items cool quickly and evenly, keeping them from becoming soggy and guaranteeing a crisp texture. Cooling racks encourage air circulation around baked goods, minimizing condensation and maintaining the quality of the finished product—whether you're baking bread, cakes, or cookies. They can also be used as a surface for frosting or glazing, which adds to their versatility and makes them an essential tool for every baker.

In summary, baking is a symphony of flavors, textures, and scents, and being prepared with the correct tools is like having a professional orchestra at your disposal. Every piece of equipment in a baker's toolset, from flexible bakeware to fine measuring tools, is essential to producing exquisite treats. The thoughtful choice of these implements improves baking and provides access to an endless supply of creative culinary possibilities. Aspiring bakers, hear our advice: get these necessary supplies and watch as your kitchen becomes an oasis of delectable options.

Key Ingredients for Festive Cookie Decorating

The aroma of freshly baked cookies fills homes as the holiday season draws near, bringing happiness and coziness. The art of decorating festive cookies is one of the most cherished customs around the Christmas season. Not only is creating delicious masterpieces out of essential sugar cookies a fun pastime, but it's also a unique way to celebrate the holiday season. This post will examine the essential components vital to the fascinating realm of holiday cookie decorating.

The base - the cookie itself - is essential to any successful cookie decorating project. A solid sugar cookie recipe serves as the foundation for this joyous custom. The perfect sugar cookie provides a canvas that accentuates the flavors of the ornamental pieces with just the right amount of buttery richness and sweetness. Although there are a gazillion recipes, the essential ingredients are usually flour, sugar, butter, eggs, and vanilla essence. This dough is easy to work with and can create various festive shapes and motifs.

Like an artist's palette, royal icing is essential to cookie decorating. Meringue powder, powdered sugar, and

water are royal icing ingredients that turn ordinary cookies into masterpieces. Its smooth texture makes elaborate detailing and spreading simple, and its short drying period guarantees that embellishments adhere firmly to the cookies. It is versatile because royal icing can be tinted with different culinary colors to create a bright spectrum for festive decorations. When working with royal icing, consistency is critical. A slightly thinner consistency works well for flooding and filling more extensive areas, while a thicker consistency works well
for outlining and creating borders.

Festive cookie decorating requires food coloring, an enchanted concoction that saturates the palette of the cookie artist. Gel-based food colors are better than liquid ones since they provide rich colors without changing the icing's consistency. With the help of these hues, bakers may create a wide range of designs, from charming pastels for springtime celebrations to classic red and green holiday patterns. Decorators may create gorgeous gradients, complex patterns, and intriguing designs that turn each cookie into a one-of-a-kind, eye-catching masterpiece with a steady hand and an excellent eye for color harmony.

Festive cookies are enhanced with edible embellishments, such as metallic paints or sprinkles. Sprinkles add a fun element and a delicious crunch. They come in a variety of forms and hues. The cookies' visual appeal is enhanced by adding texture and shine from nonpareils, sanding sugar, and dragees. Using food-grade chemicals, edible metallic paints enable designers to infuse their creations with a hint of elegance and glitz. The cookies are transformed into a visual and gastronomic spectacle, the focal point of

Christmas festivities, thanks to these decorations, which are more than just ornaments.

The unsung heroes of holiday cookie decorating, cookie cutters, play a crucial role in shaping the cookies into adorable shapes. A wide variety of cookie cutters allows you to create many creative designs, from traditional holiday forms like snowflakes and gingerbread men to more complex patterns like Christmas trees and decorations. By experimenting with various sizes and forms, bakers can produce a festive assortment of cookies that appeal to traditional and modern palates. Bakers can express their flair through decorating, which turns into a fun study of shapes and themes with the correct cookie cutter. When using cookie cutters, dip them in flour before each use to prevent the dough from sticking. Also, try to cut out shapes as close to each other as possible to minimize waste and re-rolling the dough, which can result in more challenging cookies. Like artist's brushes, intricate piping tips are indispensable for decorating biscuits with intricate details and textures. Piping tips are essential for transforming a basic cookie into a work of culinary art, outlining and creating complex patterns, or adding dimension with raised motifs. Decorators can experiment with various techniques, from delicate lines to complicated rosettes, thanks to the many tips available. Pipework is a talent that takes years to master, and decorators can hone their skills to the point where each cookie is a miniature work of beauty through practice.

Festive cookies are enhanced by the aromatic dimension that flavor extracts like peppermint, almond, or citrus bring to the sensory experience. While the essential sugar cookie offers a blank canvas, bakers can add unique flavors that capture the season's spirit using flavor extracts. Almond extract contributes a nutty richness that balances the cookie's sweetness, while peppermint extract, for instance, can transport taste receptors to a winter wonderland. These extracts are a subtle but powerful addition that enhances holiday cookies' flavor profile, making them a gourmet delight.

A more modern addition to the cookie decorator's arsenal, cookie stencils provide an easy way to access complex patterns and designs. Decorators may quickly transfer intricate pictures onto cookies with these thin, flexible sheets featuring cutout patterns. Stencils are available in many themes, from modern designs to traditional seasonal motifs, to accommodate various preferences and inclinations. Decorators can quickly create professional-looking designs with edible powders or airbrushing techniques. With cookie stencils, ease of use and creativity can coexist, allowing decorators of all skill levels to produce breathtaking creations.

To sum up, the craft of decorating festive cookies is an ode to originality, taste, and aesthetic appeal. All of the essential components of this fun project, from the basic sugar cookie to the vivid colors of food coloring, combine to make visually stunning and delicious treats. Every element—from the ease of use of cookie stencils to the accuracy of piping tips—contributes to the artistic quality of cookie decorating. Let these essential components serve as your guidance as the holiday season draws near, and you create a festive assortment of cookies that taste as good as they look. I hope the smell of freshly baked cookies fills your home and every mouthful takes you to a world of celebration and sweetness.

Tips for Successful Cookie Baking

A classic culinary practice that fills kitchens everywhere with happiness and coziness is cookie baking. Cookies are a universal favorite that cut across generational and cultural boundaries, from the traditional chocolate chip to the elaborately adorned seasonal delicacies. However, making the ideal batch of cookies can take a careful balancing act between science and creativity. This essay will go over some pointers for baking cookies successfully, focusing on the subtleties that can turn your cookies from average to extraordinary.

The quality of ingredients is a critical place to start when baking cookies. The adage "you get out what you put in" is accurate in baking. Made with premium, fresh ingredients, these cookies are delicious. Fresh eggs, premium butter, and premium flour influence the final product's texture and flavor. Keeping an eye on the ingredients' freshness can guarantee that your cookies taste better and have the right texture—chewy, crunchy, or somewhere in between.

It's critical to comprehend butter's function in cookie recipes. In addition to adding flavor, butter modifies the cookie's structure and texture. It's important to use butter at the proper temperature because softened butter incorporates sugar more efficiently and produces a smoother, more equal texture. Furthermore, the butter's temperature might impact the cookies' spread during baking. You can get the right consistency and flavor in your cookies by experimenting with different butter types and temperatures.

A key component of practical baking is accurate measuring. When working with dry substances like flour and sugar, accuracy is crucial. Using the appropriate measuring cups and spoons ensures you add the proper amount of each ingredient and avoid deviations that could result in uneven outcomes. It is advised to measure flour using the "spoon and level" approach to prevent compaction of the flour that might occur when scooping straight from the container. Precise measures impact the texture and flavor of your cookies by
balancing the ingredients.

The secret to getting the right texture in your cookies is understanding the chemistry of baking powder and baking soda. Since baking soda is alkaline, it needs an acid, such as yogurt or brown sugar, to leaven. It is frequently added in recipes when a deeper color and more intense flavor are required. However, baking powder is commonly used in recipes that call for a more neutral pH because it contains both an acid and a base. It is crucial to adhere to the recipe's instructions because adjusting the amount of these leavening ingredients can affect the cookies' texture and rise.

Chilling the cookie batter before baking can significantly improve your cookies' texture and flavor. Solidifying the lipids in the dough—especially the butter—helps the dough bake with less spread. The flavors are also concentrated when the dough is chilled, creating a more complex and subtle flavor. Chilling times can vary depending on the recipe, but the idea is always the same: letting the dough rest in the fridge before baking helps create more tasty and well-formed cookies.

Try experimenting with various sugar varieties to give your cookies more nuance and complexity. Because of its molasses content, brown sugar adds moisture and a subtle caramel flavor. White sugar provides the dish with a crisp texture and adds sweetness. To get the right balance of sweetness and texture, you can change the proportions of these sugars in a recipe. You may also experiment with other sweeteners, like honey or maple syrup, to give your cookies distinct tastes and give your baked goods a customized look.

Proper oven temperature control is essential for baking cookies that turn out well. To achieve the right texture and rise, preheating the oven guarantees that the cookies bake at the correct temperature from the outset. Precision is ensured by purchasing an oven thermometer because oven temperature precision varies. To prevent uneven browning or undercooking, rotate cookie sheets halfway through baking to ensure even cooking. Recognizing the peculiarities and characteristics of your oven enables you to adjust and produce reliable outcomes with each batch.

The correct method for portioning and shaping the dough is essential to creating the ideal cookie shape, and even baking results from size uniformity achieved with a spoon or cookie scoop. How you form the dough before baking also influences the final appearance. Your cookies will have a unique touch if you try different methods, such as shaping the dough into balls or making designs with a fork. The finished product's overall presentation and enjoyment are enhanced by its shape and appearance.

Your cookies' texture may be better if the cookie dough is over- or under-mixed. Overmixing can cause too much gluten to form, making the cookies challenging. However, undermixing could result in areas of uneven component mixture, which would change the consistency as a whole. Find the proper proportion and stir until the ingredients are incorporated to get the ideal texture in your cookies. Dry ingredients should be added gradually to the dough to ensure even distribution and avoid clumps.

Trying different add-ins is a fun way to personalize your cookies. Add-ons like chocolate chips, almonds, raisins, or seasonings can take your cookies to the next level. Remember the desired flavor profile when selecting additions and ensure they work well with the base dough. A lovely texture contrast can be achieved by experimenting with different types of chocolate and toasting nuts before adding them to the dough to enhance their flavor. There are countless ways to customize your cookies to fit various preferences and events.

The ability to tell when your cookies are done baking is something you learn through practice. Because residual heat causes cookies to continue baking after being taken out of the oven, it is best to underbake cookies to maintain their soft and chewy texture slightly. The center may still seem underdone, even if the edges should be set. The cookies will harden up as they cool on the baking sheet. You can use visual clues, like golden edges or a slight crackle on the surface, to help you figure out how long to bake anything for the best result each time.

To keep cookies fresh and flavorful, they must be stored correctly. After cookies cool fully, they should be kept in an airtight container to keep moisture and air out and maintain their texture. To assist keep the cookies from getting too dry, you can add a slice of bread to the jar. Before putting the cookies in a freezer-safe container, freeze them in a single layer for extended preservation. This extends the thrill of cookie baking beyond the first batch by enabling you to savor freshly baked cookies whenever possible.

Baking cookies successfully requires a careful balance of exact measures, premium ingredients, and systematic methods. Every stage, from the science of leavening agents to the creativity of shaping and decorating, goes into making a delicious dessert. Let these pointers serve as a roadmap for your cookie-baking endeavors, enabling you to create, experiment, and spread the delight of freshly made cookies to everyone in your vicinity. May the perfume of delicious success surround your kitchen, and everyone who indulges in your cookies finds happiness and fulfillment in each batch.

CHAPTER II

Getting Started with Basic Cookie Shapes

Introduction to Basic Cookie Shapes

Within the baking community, cookies are classic, adaptable recipes that have brought comfort and happiness to people for many years. The world of cookies is as colorful and varied as enjoyable, ranging from the traditional chocolate chip cookie to elaborately decorated sugar cookies. Every excellent cookie recipe starts with the art of shape, a crucial component that affects the finished product's texture, flavor, and aesthetic appeal. This essay takes the reader on a journey through the subtleties of common cookie forms,
examining the different approaches and factors that go into the baking process that make cookies so artistic.

Drops and circles are two of the most popular and accessible cookie shapes. These simple forms define simplicity; you only need a rudimentary concept of portioning and very little work. Round cookies are a favorite choice for many recipes, from oatmeal to chocolate chip, and are produced by shaping the dough into balls. Even baking is ensured by the round shapes, and a consistent texture is created by slightly flattening the dough balls before baking. Conversely, spoonfuls of dough are dropped straight onto the baking pan to form drop cookies. This unofficial technique yields a more rustic look and asymmetrical shapes, frequently connected to cozy, soothing foods like peanut butter cookies or Snickerdoodles.

Bar cookies are another simple shape that's a handy substitute for individual rounds or drops. The dough is evenly distributed in a baking pan to form a large slab cut into squares or bars. This approach offers a straightforward but efficient way to obtain uniform amounts without individual shaping, making it perfect for dishes like brownies, blondies, or lemon bars. Bar cookies are a favorite for get-togethers and potlucks because of how simple they make and how many they can feed.

The cutout cookie takes the stage as we get into more complex cookie shapes. This category includes a broad range of designs made by rolling out the dough and using cookie cutters to cut it into shapes. The only things restricting the possibilities are one's creativity and the wide variety of available cookie-cutter shapes. Cutout cookies provide a blank canvas for artistic creation, from traditional holiday images like snowmen and Christmas trees to commonplace forms like hearts and stars. Cutting out cookies is a meticulous process that starts with rolling the dough to the proper thickness and carefully moving the cut forms to the baking pan. The payoff is a plate of cookies that inspires the eye with their elaborate patterns and delicious taste.

Pressed cookies are cutout cookies in which the dough is shaped by passing it through a piping bag or cookie press with ornamental tips. This technique allows the creation of complex patterns and motifs without rolling and cutting. A traditional type of pressed cookie is the spritz cookie, which is famous around the holidays and frequently has delicate shapes. It takes a steady hand and knowledge of dough consistency to master the pressing technique since the dough must be flexible enough to feed through the press and maintain its shape on the baking sheet.

Rolling cookie dough into logs and cutting it into rounds offers an excellent substitute for individuals who want a denser, chewier texture. This technique, frequently applied to slice-and-bake or refrigerator cookies, enables the dough to be prepared ahead of time and provides convenient slicing and baking when needed. Before baking, the dough is sliced into rounds after being formed into a log and chilled or frozen until solid. This method guarantees that every cookie is the same size and form while also providing the option of premaking the dough.

Thumbprint cookies give the realm of cookie forms a whimsical touch. The dough is formed into balls, and the name comes from the indentation created in the center, usually with the baker's thumb. These dents act as containers for different contents, such as caramel, chocolate, or jam. The filling is tucked into the heart of each biscuit, creating a delicious fusion of flavors and sensations. In addition to being visually pleasing, thumbprint cookies offer a flavor burst that enhances the entire taste experience.

Molded cookies provide a creative outlet for individuals who enjoy novelty and have an eye for presentation. Intricate designs are imprinted onto the dough using molds or specialty cookie cutters to form these cookies. A typical example of molded cookies is the German springerle cookies. The dough is formed into cookies with engraved designs by pressing it into finely carved wooden molds. To successfully shape and bake molded cookies, precise attention to detail is necessary to maintain the integrity of the elaborate designs.

Sandwich cookies are a delicious cookie variety that consists of two cookies with a filling sandwiched in between. Each cookie can have a different shape, ranging from straightforward rounds to more complex patterns. Many filling options exist, from traditional buttercream to flavored ganache and jam. Sandwich cookies are a lovely treat, with their unique blend of flavors and textures, making every bite enjoyable. Precise assembly is required when assembling these biscuits to guarantee that the matched cookies are uniform in size and shape and produce a visually beautiful and well-balanced dessert.

In summary, cookie shaping is an art that offers a vast range of forms and techniques to experiment with, spanning both simplicity and intricacy. Every shape has unique charm and personality, from the simple round-and-drop cookies to the intricate cutout and pressed biscuits. Aspiring bakers can uncover the subtleties that add to their creations' visual appeal and flavor by experimenting with various shapes. This can provide them with a sense of accomplishment and pride. Therefore, let the creativity of cookie forms serve as your guidance while producing delicious delights that uplift and excite everyone who indulges, whether preparing traditional chocolate chip rounds or beautifully made cutout cookies.

Step-by-Step Instructions for Creating Classic Shapes

A beloved ritual that cuts across decades and countries, cookie baking entices connoisseurs into a world of flavor and inventiveness. One of the most critical aspects of this baking project is learning how to make traditional cookie forms. Each shape—from the straightforward rounds and drops to the intricate cutout and pressed cookies—requires a subtle technique to produce outstanding flavor and visual appeal. In this post, we'll look at the methods and factors of creating traditional cookie shapes that improve baking.

Round and drop cookies are a timeless classic setting the voyage's tone. For rounds, begin with a dough that has been thoroughly chilled, a crucial step to ensure that the cookies maintain their shape during baking. Using your hands, create a ball out of some of the dough, striving for uniform size. Allow ample space when placing the dough balls on a baking sheet lined with paper. To make drop cookies, distribute the dough into mounds directly onto the baking sheet using a cookie scoop or spoon. Drop cookies are a simple and quick option for home bakers due to their uneven shapes, which lend a rustic character to the cookies. Before baking, gently flatten the dough balls to achieve the desired texture and thickness. The resulting batch of cookies boasts a delightful mix of textures and a classic appearance.

Bar cookies are a favorite for many due to their simplicity and ease of preparation. Start by evenly spreading the cookie dough on a baking pan to smooth the surface. Ensuring a consistent thickness is critical to uniform baking. Once the cookie slab has been baked and cooled, cut it into bars or squares using a sharp knife. This method offers a hassle-free cookie-making approach, ideal for when time is of the essence. The versatility of bar cookies allows for the inclusion of various add-ins, like chocolate chips or nuts, enhancing
their flavor and texture.

Cutout cookies add creativity to baking, necessitating careful thought at every stage. Ensure the dough is fully refrigerated before beginning, making rolling and slicing easier. To keep the rolling pin and work surface from sticking, lightly flour them. Roll out the dough to the appropriate thickness depending on the recipe, usually between 1/4 and 1/2 inch. Select cookie cutters with designs that are whimsical or classic holiday shapes to fit the theme or occasion. Form distinct forms by pressing the cookie cutter firmly into the rolled-out dough. Leaving room between each cookie, carefully transfer the cut shapes to a baking sheet lined with parchment paper. To maintain the integrity of the shapes, it is essential to handle the dough delicately. Cutout cookies become edible canvases with royal icing, sprinkles, or other decorations once baked and chilled.

A variation on cutout cookies is that pressed cookies are made by pressing the dough through a cookie press or piping bag with ornamental tips. First, choose your preferred media or piping bag tip while considering the detailed designs it will produce. After the cookie dough has cooled down, load it into the press or bag and extrude it onto the baking sheet. Try experimenting with different tips to get a range of patterns and shapes that will give the cookies a refined appearance. Maintaining the proper consistency of the dough is essential for successful pressed cookie baking; it should be malleable enough to flow through the press or bag without losing its shape.

The first step in making these convenient slice-and-bake cookies is to form the cookie dough into a log. Starting with a cold dough will make handling it more manageable. Roll each dough's controllable sections into a log with the required diameter. Tightly cover the logs in plastic wrap and place them in the fridge to solidify. Cut the logs into rounds that are the same thickness when baking time arrives. This technique guarantees uniformly sized and shaped cookies and enables the preparation of cookie dough. Slice-and-bake cookies are a favorite among people who want ease and variety because of their adaptability to different taste profiles and add-ins.

A fun and interactive method goes into making thumbprint cookies, which are praised for their endearing look and flavorful explosion. Start by forming the cookie dough into uniformly sized balls. Make a hole in the center of each ball using your thumb or the back of a spoon. The resulting wells can be filled with anything from chocolate ganache to fruit preserves. Try various flavor combinations to see which ones work best with the original cookie. The end product is a batch of cookies that tickle the taste buds with a masterful fusion of textures and flavors, in addition to pleasing the eyes with their unique shape.

In the world of molded cookies, creativity and tradition collide. Specific molds or cookie cutters are needed to imprint elaborate patterns on the dough. Start with an adequately cooled dough and lightly flour the mold to avoid sticking. Make sure the dough adopts the beautiful design by pressing it firmly into the shape. Release the dough from the mold carefully onto the baking sheet, keeping the design intact. A typical example of molded cookies is springerle cookies, which have embossed designs that give the finished product a sophisticated touch. Paying close attention to details when shaping and baking set cookies is essential to their success.

Sandwich cookies are a lovely cookie type that provides a distinct and fulfilling baking experience. They consist of two cookies with a filling in between. Start by forming each cookie, ensuring they are all the same size. Pair them according to size and form after the cookies are made and cooled. The filling—buttercream, ganache, or jam—is sandwiched between the paired cookies, making for a delicious treat. Accuracy guarantees that the sandwiched cookies have a uniform look and balance. The end product is a decadent, aesthetically pleasing dessert that perfectly balances flavors and textures.

In summary, creating traditional cookie forms is a journey that calls for accuracy, imagination, and a passion for baking. Every form, from the straightforward rounds and drops to the intricate cutout and pressed cookies, provides a different experience for the baker and the final customer. Allow these detailed instructions to lead the way as you set out on your cookie-baking journey, offering insights into the methods and factors that go into the creativity of traditional cookie shapes. I hope the smell of freshly baked cookies fills your home and everyone who tastes them feels happy and content after they are prepared with love and care.

Troubleshooting Common Issues

Entering the realm of baking can be a pleasurable undertaking with the possibility of delicious success frequently ahead. But, like with any gastronomic journey, there are specific difficulties. Solving typical problems that arise when baking cookies is an important ability that can transform setbacks into chances for development and enhancement. This essay will examine some specific challenges bakers face and provide advice and answers to ensure your cookie-baking journey is full of successes rather than setbacks.

One familiar problem bakers face is cookies that spread out too much in the oven, becoming thin and flat. Frequently, overmixed or overly warm dough is the cause of this issue. If the cookie dough spreads too much, refrigerate it before baking. Place the cookie dough in the fridge to solidify for at least half an hour. This procedure improves the texture of the cookies while also assisting in keeping their shape. Remember to take into account the mixing time as well. Excess air introduced into the dough by overmixing might cause undesirable spreading. To avoid this problem, mix the dough until the ingredients are well incorporated.

On the other hand, bakers trying for a different texture may become frustrated with overly thick and cakey cookies. This is probably the result of using too much baking soda or flour. To solve this problem, make sure you are precisely measuring your flour and avoid overpacking by using the spoon-and-level approach. If baking soda is called for in your recipe, don't use more than is suggested. Adjusting these ingredients, you can obtain a more balanced texture with cookies that aren't excessively thick or cakey.

Another frequent problem that can lessen the overall visual attractiveness of a batch of cookies is uneven browning. Incorrectly positioned cookie sheets or erratic oven temperatures are common causes of this issue. Invest in an oven thermometer to ensure your oven reaches and holds the right temperature to address uneven browning. To guarantee that every cookie has equal exposure to the heat source, you can also achieve a more uniform bake by rotating your cookie sheets halfway through the baking process. Even baking results from evenly placed and positioned cookies on the sheet, which helps to avoid overbaking some and undercooking others.

Although surface cracks in cookies don't affect their flavor, many bakers find them unappealing. Using too much flour or overmixing the dough frequently causes these fissures. Excessive flour adds stiffness to the dough, making the baked product's flaws noticeable. Accurately measure your flour and refrain from overmixing the dough to avoid this problem. The dough should be well combined without being overdone. To lessen the appearance of any cracks in the dough, you should lightly press the dough together before baking. Dough pieces that are incorrectly shaped or proportioned can cause unevenly distributed cookies or a lopsided appearance. Consistency is essential for equal spreading and consistent shapes when portioning cookie dough. Measure equal portions of dough for each cookie using a spoon or cookie scoop. This helps ensure even baking and improves the look of your cookies. By molding each dough portion into a consistent ball or disc before baking, you may further enhance the look of your cookies and achieve a polished, eye-catching finish.

Cookies that are too crumbly or dry can be a typical problem for bakers, depriving them of the chewiness they want. Usually, overbaking or using too much flour is the culprit here. To fix this, measure your flour twice and consider lowering the quantity a little. Remember to watch the baking time as well. Dry, crumbly cookies can quickly become moist and chewy due to overbaking. When the edges of the cookies are set, but the centers are still somewhat mushy, remove them from the oven. Modify your baking time appropriately and keep a close eye on the cookies.

Conversely, undercooked and too-soft cookies can be equally annoying. Undermixing the dough or not giving it enough time to chill could cause this problem. Make sure all of the ingredients are thoroughly blended into the dough. If your recipe calls for chilling the dough before baking, follow that recommendation to give the dough's fats time to firm and minimize overspreading. Adjusting these elements can achieve cookies that achieve the ideal balance between a soft, chewy core and a moderately crisp exterior.

Efficient resolution of cookie flavor concerns necessitates meticulously evaluating ingredient composition and ratios. Should your cookies not be as sweet as you would want, go back and check how much sugar you used and modify the amounts to fit your tastes better. As an alternative, experimenting with various sugars, like maple syrup or brown sugar, can add a level of sweetness that improves the flavor profile as a whole. Make sure you are using the right kind of salt, and verify the salt measurements if the cookies taste too salty. To spread the flavor more evenly, think about using a finer salt or lowering the salt by a small amount.

In addition, cookie storage can provide difficulties for bakers. These can include excessively hard or stale cookies that lose their freshness too soon. After your cookies have cooled thoroughly, please keep them in an airtight container to preserve freshness. You can add a slice of bread to the jar to maintain moisture and keep the cookies from being too dry. If your cookies get too firm, you may soften them by putting a fresh slice of bread inside the container and letting it stay there overnight. This will allow the bread to absorb moisture. If your cookies start to get grainy, it could be because of the sugar in the recipe. Some sugars, including larger-crystal granulated sugar, might not dissolve completely in the mixing process, leaving a grainy texture. To counteract this, use finer sweets, like caster or powdered sugar, which dissolve more readily into the dough. Grittiness can also be avoided by thoroughly mixing your sugar throughout the mixing process. Because of variations in air pressure and moisture content, baking cookies at high elevations might provide particular complications. Cookies may spread, rise too quickly, or dry out more rapidly at higher altitudes. Modifying your recipe to consider these things if you want the intended outcomes is essential. To achieve the ideal balance, consider lowering the leavening agent dosage, raising the liquid content, or experimenting with flour modifications. Baking at a slightly lower temperature at high elevations also helps produce better results.

In conclusion, prospective bakers must learn how to fix typical cookie challenges. Comprehending the subtleties of every issue and its possible resolutions improves your baking skills and converts obstacles into chances for development and improvement. Let each obstacle you overcome on your journey through the baking world serve as a springboard for a deeper comprehension of the technique and science involved in making the ideal cookies. May the sweet scent of accomplishment fill your kitchen, and everyone who tastes your delicious cookies feel happy and fulfilled after each batch.

CHAPTER III

Advanced Festive Shapes

Exploring Intricate and Unique Cookie Designs

Within the magical world of baking, cookies are like little canvases, begging to be filled with food and created into masterpieces. Beyond the realm of straightforward forms and timeless patterns, there is a world of sophisticated and distinctive cookie design, where bakers transform into artisans, and each cookie is an expression of their talent and imagination. In this essay, we will investigate the methods, resources, and sources of inspiration that turn cookie decorating into a culinary art.

A nicely shaped and baked canvas is frequently the first step in creating an intricate cookie design. The creative process begins with selecting cookie dough, whether a traditional sugar cookie or a tasty gingerbread. The dough must be rolled appropriately out and chilled for complex forms and designs to stay intact during baking—consistency in dough thickness between cookies guarantees uniform baking and a unified appearance. The flavor and texture of a cookie are in perfect proportion, making them the ideal canvas for creative embellishments.

The ideal material for elaborate cookie decoration turns out to be royal icing. Made with powdered sugar, meringue powder, and water, royal icing has a silky texture ideal for fine details and complex designs. Because of how quickly it dries, embellishments adhere to the cookies securely, giving delicate designs or extra layers of support. The versatility of royal icing makes it so beautiful; it can be colored with a wide range of food colors, allowing bakers to create eye-catching designs that make biscuits come to life.

Knowledge of color theory and skill are necessary for coloring royal icing. Gel-based food coloring is the better option because of its concentrated pigments, which guarantee vivid colors without diluting the consistency of the icing. Finding the ideal color balance is a craft; harmonious palettes, contrasting tones, and subtle gradients enhance the finished design's visual attractiveness. Bakers frequently use color combinations to convey particular feelings or themes, turning their cookies into artistic works.

Regarding elaborate cookie design, piping bags and various tips become the artist's brushes. Piping tips are available in multiple sizes and forms, and each has a distinct function in producing patterns and textures. The star tip adds complexity with its rough appearance, while the round tip is perfect for outlining and creating fine details. Floral designs are enhanced by leaf and petal tips, and a flat tip works well for covering more extensive regions with icing. The ability to pipe well, from simple lines to elaborate rosettes, takes effort and patience.

When it comes to creating elaborate cookie designs, flood icing offers many options beyond the limitations of standard piping techniques. Because it's significantly thinner than regular icing, flood icing works well to cover more significant areas and smooth surfaces. This method makes it possible to overlay fine details on top, create gradient effects, and blend colors seamlessly. To flood, first, outline the area to be attacked and then carefully spread the thinner icing inside the lines. The end effect is a polished, faultless surface that provides the background for more intricate embellishments.

Food-safe markers and edible paints provide extra tools for sophisticated cookie design, enabling freehand painting and drawing on the cookies. Edible metallic paints give the designs a hint of glitz and refinement because they are manufactured with substances fit for eating. Like fine-tipped pens, food-safe markers offer accuracy and convenience for drawing delicate lines and details. With these instruments, bakers may express themselves more fully and give their cookies a distinctive artistic touch.

A more modern addition to the cookie decorator's arsenal, cookie stencils provide an easy way to access complex patterns and designs. Decorative artists may quickly transfer intricate motifs onto cookies with the help of these thin, flexible sheets with cutout designs. Stencils are available in many themes, from modern designs to traditional seasonal motifs, to accommodate various preferences and inclinations. Decorators can quickly create professional-looking designs with edible powders or airbrushing techniques. With cookie stencils, ease of use and creativity can coexist, allowing decorators of all skill levels to produce breathtaking creations.

Intricate cookie designs heavily rely on texture to give the composition depth and visual appeal. Before baking, cookie dough can be decorated with elaborate patterns using impression tools, embossing mats, and textured rolling pins. These tools imprint patterns that range from fanciful textures to delicate lace patterns, turning a bare surface into an eye-catching environment. Every cookie is a one-of-a-kind, tactile work of art because of how the various textures interact to highlight the intricacy of the pattern.

Often, intricate cookie designs incorporate three-dimensional components in addition to surface-level motifs. Fondant is a soft, flexible material that resembles frosting that sculptors use to create complex decorations. By shaping fondant into elaborate features, figures, or flowers, bakers can give their sweets a sculptural quality. The combination of royal icing and fondant creates intricate, multi-layered decorations that transform cookies into stunning, mouthwatering masterpieces.

There's no better source of inspiration for elaborate cookie designs than nature. Cookies with floral themes have an air of sophistication and eternal beauty derived from detailed foliage and blossoming blossoms. The natural world's inhabitants, such as birds and butterflies, offer countless inspirations for imaginative and captivating designs. Decorators may bring the outdoors to life on a small, edible canvas by utilizing the subtle nuances found in nature as a playground.

Holidays and celebrations provide rich subject material for intricately designed cookies. Decorators can create cookies with themes for birthdays or weddings or use festive holiday motifs. The skill of designing elaborate cookies enables the production of delectable centerpieces.

Techniques for Achieving Complex Shapes

In the fascinating realm of cookie baking, a baker's ability to create intricate shapes reflects their talent, accuracy, and imagination. Beyond simple squares and circles, cookies can have complex, ornate designs that turn them into tasty art pieces. In this essay, we will look closer at the procedures that turn dough into delicious, elaborate works of art and the tactics and approaches that enable bakers to become experts in crafting intricate cookie designs.

Selecting an appropriate cookie dough is the first step toward creating intricate cookie forms. While traditional sugar cookies offer a flexible foundation, several recipes add other ingredients to improve the dough's flavor and workability. Cream cheese and sour cream give the dough moisture and tenderness, making it more flexible and straightforward. Finding the right balance between the dough's firmness and flexibility is crucial for maintaining the shape of the finished product during baking.

An even cookie dough layer must be rolled out before intricate shapes may be achieved. Rolling pin rings or spacers aid in preserving a uniform thickness throughout the dough sheet. This guarantees that every cookie bakes consistently, no matter how shaped, avoiding uneven textures or overbaking in some spots. Accurately rolling out the dough helps achieve the right texture and uniformity and improves the end product's appearance. The correct tools and methods are needed to cut rolled-out dough into complicated shapes. Cookie cutters are available in various sizes and shapes, from straightforward geometric patterns to intricately themed cutters. Purchasing specialist or custom-made cutters offers a customized approach to cookie design for more intricate forms. Furthermore, crisp, defined lines are made easier with a sharp-edged cookie cutter, which produces cookies that hold their shape during baking. Some bakers use metal cutters, which help to create a nice edge on the cookies and conduct heat evenly.

An alternative way to create complex shapes is with cookie dough templates, mainly when fine detailing is involved. These food-safe plastic or cardboard templates serve as a stencil for the intended shape, directing the cutting process. Bakers can use a knife or a smaller cutter to trace around the borders of the template once it is placed on the rolled-out dough. More control and accuracy are available with this technique, especially when working with intricate or multi-layered designs.

To achieve intricate shapes, it's common practice to layer several dough colors to produce eye-catching patterns. Cookie marbling is a technique that adds swirls and complex designs to the dough, similar to methods used in painting and pottery. Doughs of various colors can be combined and gently kneaded or rolled together by bakers to create a marbled look that gives the finished shapes depth and visual appeal. This method improves the cookies' appearance while offering a pleasant surprise when they are nibbled, exposing the subtle details of the marbled design.

Transferring the cut dough forms to the baking sheet is a delicate task that takes skill for cookies with cutout designs or detailed cutwork. Lifting and moving the cut objects without causing distortion is made easier with the help of an offset spatula or a thin, flexible spatula.

The cut shapes retain structural integrity during careful maneuvering if they are briefly frozen before being transferred to the baking sheet. Achieving complicated cookie designs mostly depends on ensuring a meticulous and seamless transfer of complex shapes.

Using cookie cutters that are 3D printed has become a cutting-edge method for creating precise details on complex forms. Bakers and designers can produce custom cutters with elaborate designs that are difficult to do with conventional techniques. Food-grade materials are used to make these cutters, guaranteeing safety and enabling the creation of intricate and distinctive shapes. By pushing the limits of what is possible with conventional tools, bakers can experiment with novel cookie designs thanks to the precision provided by 3D-printed cutters.

Another way to create complicated shapes, especially ones with sculptural aspects or fine details, is by using baking molds. Silicone molds, in particular, are becoming increasingly well-liked due to their versatility and simplicity. By pressing cookie dough into these molds, bakers can replicate intricate patterns or motifs that could be difficult to produce with conventional cutters. The molds are designed to capture complex textures and shapes, resulting in cookies that are not only aesthetically pleasing but also have a refined and expertly finished appearance.

Complex forms can be achieved with mechanical precision thanks to cookie presses. Bakers may easily make consistent shapes with fine detail using this portable equipment with removable discs exhibiting numerous designs. Cookie presses are popular for festive occasions or events when efficiency and precision are crucial since they are especially well-suited to creating big batches of cookies with a uniform appearance.

The process of cookie embossing lends elegance to the finished design when working with intricate shapes. Embossing is pressing a pattern or design into the cookie dough before baking. Textured rolling pins or specialty embossing mats can be used for this. Adding a tactile element to the overall experience, the intricate patterns created by embossing result in visually stunning cookies with raised decoration. Because embossing techniques are so flexible, bakers can try out a variety of textures and patterns to fit their creative vision.

Completing intricate forms goes beyond baking and involves decorating and adding the last details that make cookies come to life. Royal icing serves as the artist's palette, enabling the application of deft decorations, thin lines, and detailed information. Using piping bags with tiny tips, decorators can draw shapes, add complex patterns, and

Inspirational Ideas for Festive Occasions

We all have a special place for festive occasions because they catalyze happiness, community, and celebration. These occasions, whether religious holidays, cultural celebrations, or personal anniversaries, offer us the chance to make enduring memories and deepen our connections. This essay will go over several creative ideas that you can use to make your holiday gatherings even more special and unforgettable.

Embracing diversity and cultural complexity is one of the most meaningful ways to inspire celebratory events. Festivals, which highlight distinctive traditions, customs, and rituals, can act as windows into the colorful tapestry of many nations. Consider planning a cultural exchange where relatives and friends can share food, dancing, and music from their homeland. This develops a greater awareness and respect for the world we live in and strengthens our sense of unity.

Festivities that inspire come from the strength of giving back to the community. Consider including deeds of kindness and charity in the festivities rather than just personal celebrations. Plan a volunteer event where people may give their time and energy to a worthwhile cause. This promotes the idea that festivities should uplift the community and bring people together in a spirit of goodwill.

Moreover, when organizing celebrations, one should pay attention to the transformational potential of creativity. Adding a creative touch to every celebration gives a memorable and personal touch, whether by creating distinctive themed costumes, bespoke invites, or venue decorations with handcrafted ornaments. Inspire your guests to work on do-it-yourself projects to develop a spirit of creativity and teamwork beyond typical celebrations.

When it comes to celebrations, food is essential. Rather than following the typical menu selections, investigate international culinary customs. Organize a potluck dinner where each attendee contributes a dish that symbolizes their home culture. This offers a way for gastronomic exploration and appreciation in addition to diversifying and thrilling the dining experience.

Furthermore, celebrations might benefit from the inspiration that narrative can bring. Write a story that connects the past, present, and future and ties the celebration to a more prominent topic. Tell personal tales, anecdotes, or cultural myths that have meaning for the event to establish a feeling of continuity and importance. This narrative component gives the celebration more excellent substance and elevates it beyond a moment.

The embrace of the natural world and the surroundings is another source of inspiration for celebratory events. Think about having parties outside in the breathtaking scenery. This encourages a closer bond with nature and offers a welcome change of pace. Plan outdoor games, tree-planting ceremonies, or other events that let people interact with nature to foster a joyful, environmentally responsible, and inspiring ambiance.
Furthermore, there's no denying that music can elevate celebratory events. Select songs that fit the celebration's theme to create a soundtrack that makes the event more enjoyable. Live performances may add a vibrant and engaging element to the festivities and leave a lasting impact on all those in attendance, whether professional musicians or gifted visitors perform.

Celebrations can benefit from the creative infusion of technology in the digital age. Think of adding virtual components, such as live-streaming the celebration for loved ones who live far away or making a digital scrapbook that contains the best moments from the occasion. This broadens the celebration's audience and incorporates contemporary tools into customary celebrations, making for an unforgettable and one-of-a-kind event.

Moreover, practicing mindfulness and introspection can enrich celebratory events with deep inspiration. Incorporate gratitude activities, meditation, or quiet times to let attendees connect with their inner selves and understand the occasion's significance. This contemplative component gives the celebrations more depth and promotes attention beyond the evident excitement.

Finally, there is an endless supply of inspiration during celebrations. Celebrations can go above and beyond the usual by embracing diversity, giving back to the community, letting creativity run wild, experimenting with culinary customs, including storytelling, spending time in nature, utilizing music and technology, and encouraging mindfulness. Let these motivational thoughts create a vivid and enduring impression on our joyous occasions as we travel the fabric of our lives, making every moment a treasured memory.

CHAPTER IV

The Art of Sugar Sprinkles

Understanding the Variety of Sugar Sprinkles

Sugar sprinkles are those vibrant, tiny crystals that give baked goods a pop of sweetness and flare. They have become a staple in the culinary industry. Sugar sprinkles are more than just decorations; they are available in various sizes, styles, and flavors, providing bakers and hobbyists with a wide range of options. In this investigation, we explore the intriguing world of sugar sprinkles, looking at their various varieties, the production methods that go into them, and the inventive ways they may improve the flavor and appearance of our favorite baked goods.

The vast array of varieties and hues drives the popularity of sugar sprinkles. The selection is enormous and constantly changing, ranging from traditional rainbow assortments to specialty mixes with holiday themes. Of the countless options available to bakers, sanding sugar, nonpareils, jimmies, and dragees are just a few examples. With its giant crystals, sanding sugar gives cookies and cupcakes a wonderful crunch and a pop of color. Conversely, nonpareils are tiny, spherical sprinkles that add a touch of color and a delicate texture. Longer and thinner than nonpareils, jimmies are ideal for bringing a whimsical element to frosted cakes and ice cream sundaes. Dragees, tiny metallic balls, provide a sophisticated and wealthy appearance perfect for wedding cakes and other high-end delicacies.

Just as fascinating as the variety of sugar sprinkles is their manufacturing procedure. These little treats are made primarily of sugar crystals, which are processed to create several types of sprinkles by varying their size and texture. For example, more giant sugar crystals are crushed into tiny bits to create sanding sugar, which has a coarser texture. Small sugar beads are extruded to form nonpareils coated in vivid hues. Jimmies are made by pushing sugar paste through a nozzle to give them their distinctive elongated shape. Dragees are made by piling sugar around a core and then covering it with a thin layer of gold or silver. These candies are frequently pearlized or metallic in appearance.

Another feature of sugar sprinkles that appeals to bakers and customers is their color scheme. Classic rainbow assortments are ageless and adaptable, perfect for various events. However, the range of colors has grown with the introduction of natural food dyes, providing more vivid and subtle choices. Now that multiple tints are available, bakers can match sprinkles to particular themes, seasons, or branding requirements. These shades range from pastel hues to deep, rich tones. How color options for sugar sprinkles have changed throughout time reflects the ever-expanding demand for visually spectacular confections and the dynamic nature of culinary aesthetics.

Sugar sprinkles add to baked goods' whole flavor experience and visual attractiveness. The quantity and kind of sprinkles can affect the texture, adding a nice crunch or a delicate sweetness pop. With its giant crystals, sanding sugar offers a delightful crunch in contrast to the softness of cookies or the smoothness of frosting. Because they are softer and smaller than parsley, nonpareils add a subtle tactile aspect without overpowering the taste. While dragees, with its thin sugar covering, add a gentle sweetness that balances the dessert's underlying flavors, jimmies' flavor is reminiscent of beloved childhood favorites.

Beyond the customary applications of sugar sprinkles for adorning cookies and cupcakes, inventive bakers are developing novel methods to use these tiny crystals in a wide range of confections. Sprinkles are a fashionable fad for rimming glasses for celebratory drinks. The vivid hues give milkshakes, mocktails, and cocktails a visually pleasing touch. Cake pops dusted with sprinkles and strawberries dipped in chocolate demonstrate the versatility of these candy embellishments. Additionally, bakers are experimenting with incorporating sprinkles directly into the dough to create cakes and sweets that resemble confetti that surprise and delight with every mouthful.

In addition, sugar sprinkles are already a common sight in the rapidly developing field of culinary art. Talented bakers use these tiny crystals to create edible wonders, ranging from elaborate cookie decorations to intricate cake patterns. The popularity of customized sprinkle mixes, which enable unique color schemes and themes, has stimulated bakers' imaginations. A new generation of bakers is being inspired to explore the artistic possibilities of sugar sprinkles by the abundance of visually spectacular products on social media platforms that showcase these custom mixtures of sprinkles.

To sum up, the world of sugar sprinkles is colorful and diverse, providing a wide range of options for novice and expert bakers. There is no limit to what may be created in the culinary arts thanks to the diversity of varieties

and colors available, from the traditional rainbow assortments to specialty dragees and custom mixes. Knowing how sugar sprinkles are made offers a new level of appreciation for these tiny crystals that are now associated with gluttony and celebration. Sugar sprinkles prove that even the most minor details can significantly impact the flavor and appearance of our favorite baked goods as cooks continue to push the bounds of inventiveness. Thus, the next time you grab that jar of sugar sprinkles, remember that you are
opening up a world of limitless possibilities and sensory pleasure rather than merely decorating your cake.

Creative Ways to Use Sprinkles for Decoration

Sprinkles aren't just for the tops of cupcakes or the edges of cookies—they're such fun confectionary decorations. Sprinkles have evolved into valuable baking and creative cooking tools, providing many options beyond the conventional sprinkle-on-top method. This essay looks at the inventive ways sprinkles can be used to decorate cakes, turning them into aesthetically pleasing and delicious delights.

Using sprinkles to the actual texture of the cake is one creative method to use them. Sprinkles are no longer just for the top; bakers incorporate them into batters, doughs, and mixes to create visually appealing and delicious treats. Every slice of a cake made in a funfetti manner, with sprinkles included in the batter, is a colorful explosion. The rainbow-hued confetti-like speckles elevate the cake, transforming an otherwise unremarkable dessert into a visual and palatable feast, and likewise, adding sprinkles to cookie dough before baking yields delicious cookies with a fun and whimsical look.

In addition, sprinkles have made their way into the beverage industry, giving drinks a whimsical touch. Sprinkles have become a popular way to decorate the rims of glasses, especially during celebratory events. The flavors of milkshakes, mocktails, and cocktails go well with the vivid hues and textures of the sprinkles. This inventive application of sprinkles shows how these small candies may improve the aesthetic appeal of various culinary dishes, taking the concept of decoration outside of the baked goods domain.

Another creative way to utilize sprinkles is on cake pops, those little treats on a stick. Sprinkles are now being embedded in cake pops by bakers instead of just adorning the outside. The end product is a delicacy that, in addition to having a vibrant surface, delights the taste with beautiful bursts of sweetness upon discovering the embedded sprinkles with every mouthful. This fun take on a well-known dessert demonstrates how sprinkles can be more than just a decorative element for culinary experiences.

Sprinkles are revolutionizing the visual appeal of chocolate-dipped snacks by taking center stage and enhancing the visual appeal of pretzels, strawberries, and other treats. Bakers produce visually appealing textures and patterns by coating dipped dishes with various sprinkles, improving the overall appearance. These decadent delights have a sensory element that appeals to the eyes and the palate because of the contrast between the crisp, colorful sprinkles and the velvety chocolate covering.

A unique and personalized method to utilize sprinkles for decoration is with custom sprinkle mixes. Bakers and connoisseurs can create special mixes by blending various hues, forms, and sizes to fit particular themes or events. This personalization gives baked goods an extra dimension of inventiveness beyond what can be achieved with premade sprinkle assortments. Custom sprinkle mixes have become a must-have for those looking to add a unique and customized visual identity to their work.

Sprinkles are now a necessary instrument in culinary art for producing elaborate and eye-catching designs. To realize their culinary fantasies, talented bakers use a variety of sprinkles to create intricate cake decorations and cookie designs. Sprinkles can create precise and artistic details in floral arrangements, geometric patterns, and portraits. Their vibrant and tiny size makes them an excellent tool for showcasing creative talent. Many incredible works on social media demonstrate the endless possibilities of using sprinkles as an artistic medium in the realm of edible art.

Another creative way to use sprinkles is during holidays and special occasion celebrations. Desserts are made more festive with themed sprinkle decorations, which are made to fit various seasons or occasions. Sprinkles can be utilized to enhance the theme and mood of any occasion. Examples are Halloween delicacies covered with bat-shaped sprinkles, Christmas cookies powdered with snowflake sprinkles, and birthday cakes adorned with jubilant confetti mixtures. Bakers can add a festive and joyful touch to their dishes by personalizing sprinkle selections according to the occasion.

In addition, the technique of stacking and blending various sprinkle varieties provides an elegant way to decorate. Bakers are layering sprinkles of different sizes and shapes in an experiment to produce textured and multidimensional designs. This careful process turns baked delicacies into tiny works of art by giving their visual appeal more depth and complexity. These tiered sprinkle decorations demonstrate the countless ways to exhibit creativity and artistry in baking through the interplay of colors and textures.

In conclusion, many inventive methods of using sprinkles as decoration go far beyond the traditional practice of just sprinkling them over sweets. Bakers are displaying the versatility of these little confections by incorporating them into recipes and doughs, rimming glasses, embedding them within cake pops, and making unique sprinkle mixes. In the hands of culinary artisans, sprinkles have evolved into indispensable tools that enable them to create aesthetically spectacular and singularly delightful delicacies. Sprinkles are proof positive that even seemingly insignificant elements can significantly impact the appearance and flavor of our favorite pastries as the baking industry develops. Thus, the next time you grab a jar of sprinkles, investigate how these small candies can transform your creations into edible artwork using your imagination.

Tips for Perfect Sprinkle Application

The careful nuances of presentation are just as much a part of the baking and cooking arts as the actual component combinations. The sprinkle application is one such element that frequently transforms a dish from ordinary to spectacular. How you use sprinkles can significantly impact the ultimate visual appeal of your creation, whether you're decorating a cake, cookies, or cupcakes. In this post, we'll look at a few techniques for getting the ideal sprinkle application so that your gourmet creations taste as good as they taste.

To begin with, knowing how texture functions is essential to getting a perfect sprinkle application. Whether you're using glaze on a donut or icing on a cake, the texture of your foundation will affect how effectively the sprinkles stick to it and display their brilliant colors. A slightly tacky but smooth surface makes the perfect canvas for distributing and securing sprinkles uniformly. The sprinkles may not stick if the surface is arid, resulting in an uneven dispersion and a dull appearance.

Color scheme consideration is as important as texture consideration for a sprinkle application to be visually pleasing. Colors that contrast or match can significantly impact how your food looks overall. For instance, chocolate sprinkles can make a sophisticated contrast on a surface painted in pastel colors, while colorful rainbow sprinkles can go well with plain white icing. You can showcase your creativity and customize the appearance of your food to fit a particular theme or occasion by experimenting with color combinations.

Achieving the intended impression also heavily depends on the size and shape of the sprinkles. More giant sprinkles, such as jimmies or nonpareils, can give your design a striking and dynamic touch. On the other hand, finer sprinkles, such as edible glitter or sanding sugar, appear more polished and delicate. By selecting the ideal combination for your dish, you can improve its overall appearance by being aware of the visual impact of various sprinkle sizes.

Another essential element in reaching excellence is placing sprinklers precisely. To produce a well-balanced and aesthetically beautiful pattern, think about strategically placing the sprinkles rather than randomly dispersing them throughout the surface. With the deliberate placement of each sprinkle, you may construct borders, patterns, or even complex designs. This degree of attention to detail highlights your commitment to culinary presentation and enhances the dish's visual impact.

Timing is essential when adding sprinkles to a cake or other baked items. If you sprinkle too soon, the colors may run due to the base's dampness, causing sinking or bleeding. However, if you wait too long, the surface can dry up and make it easier for the sprinkles to adhere, which would result in poor adhesion. Selecting the best time to sprinkle depends on the recipe and the surrounding circumstances. This will guarantee a perfect coating that will improve the appearance of your dish as a whole.

Another crucial part of applying sprinkles is taking dietary limitations into account. It's critical to pay attention to the ingredients in your sprinkles due to the rise in dietary preferences and food sensitivities. Selecting vegan or allergen-free sprinkles enables you to serve a larger audience while maintaining an eye-catching look. Building trust and inclusion with your customers is another benefit of being open and honest about the ingredients in your sprinkles. For example, if you're catering to a vegan audience, sprinkles free from gelatin and other animal-derived ingredients. If serving customers with food allergies, choose sprinkles free from common allergens like nuts and gluten.

In summary, attaining the ideal sprinkle application calls for several elements that enhance the overall visual appearance of your food preparations. The little things—like realizing how vital texture is, thinking about color schemes, playing with sprinkle sizes, and perfecting placement—significantly impact how beautiful your food looks. You can transform typical snacks into unique culinary artwork by paying attention to these pointers and using them in your baking and cooking initiatives. After all, the pleasure of enjoying tasty food is only
enhanced when it is served with the attention to detail and originality that come with a well-applied sprinkling.

CHAPTER V

Decorating Techniques for Beginners

Easy and Fun Decorating Techniques

In culinary arts, a dish's presentation is as important as its flavor. Decorating techniques give baked goods an additional creative layer that transforms them into aesthetically striking works of art. For inexperienced and seasoned bakers, the world of superficial and enjoyable decorating techniques offers many options for anything from cakes and cupcakes to cookies and pastries.

The traditional cupcake decorating method of swirling icing is one of the easiest yet most effective techniques. Anyone can create gorgeous and alluring swirls that instantly improve the appearance of a cupcake with just a piping bag and a star tip. For bakers of all skill levels, experimenting with different frosting colors and textures yields countless variants, making it a versatile and fun method. Its simplicity makes it beautiful, demonstrating that sometimes less is more regarding décor.

There are endless options available to individuals who want to give their baked goods a sophisticated touch through the skill of pipetting elaborate designs using royal icing. Royal icing gives precise embellishments the flexibility and precision they need, from exquisite flowers on birthday cakes to delicate lace designs on wedding pastries. Although it could take some time to get the hang of it, the results are worth it because it lets bakers add beautiful and distinctive designs to their products.

Edible flowers and herbs are another fun decoration idea that enhances visual appeal and gives food a hint of flavor. Cakes and sweets can be adorned with candied violets, pansies, or rose petals for a classy and organic look. Fresh herbs, such as basil or mint, can be thoughtfully arranged to improve the dish's overall appearance and taste. Each dish is transformed into a botanical beauty by using edible flowers, which adds a touch of the garden to the kitchen.

Fondant sculpting is an endless creative outlet for bakers who like to incorporate whimsical and whimsical elements into their creations. It is possible to shape fondant, a malleable sugar paste, into complex forms, characters, and three-dimensional embellishments. Fondant sculpture lets bakers realize their creative vision, from cute animals on birthday cakes to elaborate wedding cake toppers. The satisfaction of watching edible sculptures come to life is a treat in and of itself, even though it could call for a steady touch and a little creative flare.

Another easy way to give baked goods a sophisticated touch is to stencil them. Stencils can create detailed patterns and motifs on the surface of cakes, pastries, and sweets using powdered sugar, cocoa, or edible spray. Stenciling's adaptability opens them to a world of possibilities, ranging from contemporary geometric motifs to traditional damask patterns. Bakers may effortlessly obtain a glossy, professional design that catches the eye without sacrificing simplicity by adding stencils to their toolkit.

The technique of marbling provides an aesthetically pleasing yet surprisingly easy way to decorate cakes and sweets. Bakers may make stunning designs that resemble marble by swirling together various colored fondants or batters. This method offers infinite color combinations and variants, adding a sense of refinement. Marbling provides a dramatic and creative element to baked goods that will wow the eyes and the taste buds, whether one uses bright, vibrant hues or subtle pastels.

The popularity of drip cakes, which offer a chic and eye-catching decorating method, has swept the baking community in recent years. Cake edges get drippings of colorful icing or ganache, which adds a striking and contemporary appearance. Drip cakes are incredibly versatile; the color and consistency of the drips can create a robust and fun look or an elegant, minimalist one. This method adds a delectably rich touch to the entire presentation while offering a distinctive and visually striking way to highlight innovation.

Incorporating edible glitter or metallic dust is a simple yet effective approach to enhance texture, essential for baked goods' visual appeal. Edible glitter and dust are a great way to add sparkle to cupcakes or a stunning metallic finish to a cake. They also make desserts look more elegant and sophisticated. Moderation is crucial; a hint of sparkle gives a magical touch without overpowering the entire design. This method is especially well-liked for formal events where a little glitz is appreciated, including weddings and festivals.

In conclusion, the world of decorating techniques is more than just a tool for improving the visual attractiveness of baked goods. It's also a platform for bakers to express their unique creativity and add a personal touch to their culinary products. From basic frosting swirls to complex royal icing designs, each technique allows bakers to put a piece of themselves into their creations. There's nothing more satisfying than knowing that the beautiful and visually striking displays you've created are pleasing to the eye and reflect your unique style and personality.

Hands-On Activities for Novice Decorators

For inexperienced bakers, diving into cake creation and culinary artistry may be exhilarating and intimidating. The want to produce aesthetically pleasing delicacies frequently coexists with needing help figuring out where to start. However, there are many practical projects designed for inexperienced decorators that make learning easier and encourage creativity in the kitchen. For those eager to turn their culinary projects into edible works of art, these activities offer a solid foundation, from learning the fundamentals of piping to exploring fondant sculpting and cookie decorating.

For any budding designer, piping—applying ornamental components with a pastry bag—is a necessary talent. Beginner bakers should begin by mastering the fundamental piping methods, which include shells, stars, and rosettes. These basic patterns are adaptable and can be used as the basis for more complex ornamentation. Decorators can become more comfortable using a pastry bag and managing the icing flow by practicing with buttercream or royal icing. Decorators can move on to more complex piping techniques, such as borders, flowers, and intricate patterns, as their skill level increases. Piping is a hands-on activity that improves motor skills and gives decorators a sense of satisfaction as they see their creations come to life.

Novice decorators can explore three-dimensional culinary art through fondant sculpting. Fondant is a soft sugar paste perfect for shaping and molding into various shapes, making it an excellent material for cake toppers and edible sculptures. Before moving on to more complex patterns like animals or figurines, beginners might begin with primary forms like flowers or bows. Decorating with fondant gives decorators a tactile experience that lets them experiment with their creative impulses. Mastering fondant sculpting may take time and practice, but the reward is an aesthetically stunning artwork demonstrating talent and imagination.

Cookie decorating is a practical craft that blends the artistic expression of design with the delight of baking. Decorators can experiment with techniques like flooding, piping, and decorating with edible decorations, using sugar cookies as a blank canvas. To decorate cookies, beginners first learn how to flood cookies, which involves using royal icing to create a uniform, smooth surface. Decorators can progress to more complex patterns, such as layered decorations and delicate piped detailing, as their confidence improves. Cookie decorating gives new decorators a fun and tasty opportunity to showcase their creativity by allowing them to play with different colors, textures, and patterns.

Cake pops are bite-sized candies on a stick that provide new decorators with an enjoyable and manageable start to edible creation. These little round cakes are a versatile and fun DIY project that can be embellished with sprinkles and dipped in colorful candy melts. To create a range of aesthetically pleasing sweets, novice decorators can experiment with different cake pop flavors, coatings, and ornamental features. Cake pop shape, dipping, and decorating are enjoyable, hands-on activities that provide positive results. It is an excellent place for beginners to start if they are interested in edible art because it allows for a fun and relaxed atmosphere for them to hone their decorating talents.

A traditional and popular hobby, decorating cupcakes provides a smaller canvas for inexperienced decorators to exhibit their creativity. Cupcakes are the ideal size to test different icing methods, hues, and topping combinations. For a basic yet gorgeous design, novice decorators might begin by learning how to swirl buttercream onto cupcakes. Decorators can experiment with more sophisticated methods as their confidence improves, such as piping detailed flowers, producing ombre effects, or using textured toppings. For inexperienced decorators, cupcake decorating classes or online tutorials offer a wealth of advice, including clear directions and ideas for producing aesthetically pleasing and delectable sweets.

Chocolate sculpting is a tactile craft that blends the luxurious and decadent world of chocolate with decoration. Inexperienced decorators might experiment with melting and tempering chocolate to make molded shapes like hearts, flowers, or unique designs. Decorators can add a creative element to the process by experimenting with different chocolate flavors and colors using chocolate molds. Chocolate molding is a tactile art that stimulates the senses and the imagination because it is a hands-on process. This project enables inexperienced decorators to explore chocolate creativity with delectable and eye-catching results, whether making decorations for cakes or individual delights.

Cake stenciling is a hands-on pastime that adds elaborate decorations to cakes and pastries for people who value presentation art. Cakes can have their surfaces stenciled with edible dust or icing to produce intricate patterns and designs. The stencils are constructed of ingredients that are safe for consumption. As their abilities improve, inexperienced decorators can begin with basic stencils and work up to more complex designs. Cake stenciling offers decorators a distinctive and creative method to accentuate baked goods' visual
appeal. They can use colors, textures, and patterns to produce eye-catching and customized masterpieces.

Finally, practical exercises designed for inexperienced decorators offer a fun and approachable way to get started in edible art. Through these activities, prospective decorators can explore their creativity in the kitchen and learn everything from the fundamentals of piping to fondant modeling and cookie decorating, among other things. These tactile encounters help to improve motor skills and give inexperienced decorators a sense of success when they see their creations come to life. For both new bakers and decorators, these hands-on activities set the stage for a pleasant and satisfying journey into decoration, whether through creating edible sculptures, designing delicate biscuits, or experimenting with chocolate artistry.

Building Confidence in Cookie Decorating

More than just a cooking hobby, cookie decorating is a fun, edible art that lets people express their imagination and give baked items a magical touch. Decorating cookies with elaborate designs may be daunting and thrilling for many people. Nonetheless, anyone can gain confidence in cookie decorating and transform essential sugar cookies into delectable works of art with the appropriate strategy and some practice.

Understanding the fundamentals is essential to developing confidence while decorating cookies. Start with a tried-and-true sugar cookie recipe that bakes into a sturdy canvas to support your creative endeavors. Comprehending uniformity's significance in cookie dough and frosting is vital for attaining neat and polished designs. A uniform thickness for the rolled-out dough guarantees even baking, and the appropriate icing thickness enables flawless application and accurate detailing.

Now that you know the basics, it's time to explore the realm of royal icing, the preferred decorating method for cookies. Because royal icing has a glossy, smooth texture, it's ideal for flooding cookies and producing a beautiful base. Here, too, consistency is crucial. The best outcomes are guaranteed when the thickness is just suitable—thin enough to flow easily but thick enough to maintain shape. Please spend some time honing the technique of flooding, which involves icing biscuits in a base layer and letting it set before adding detailed decorations.

The foundation of cookie decorating is piping methods; becoming proficient with them is a big step toward gaining confidence. To get comfortable using a piping bag, start with basic designs like dots, lines, and swirls. Gradually advance to more intricate methods to give your designs depth and dimension, like flooding and outlining. The secret is to practice frequently and accept that mistakes are necessary for learning. Thanks to better control and muscle memory, your piping skills will develop with time.

You can create many different effects by experimenting with separate piping bag tips. Although a round tip works well for flooding and outlining, specialty tips such as petal or star tips can give your drawings more depth and variation. You may adapt your decorations to particular themes or events by knowing the effects of various recommendations. Feel free to combine different tips to make your cookies have interesting and eye-catching patterns.

In cookie decorating, color is essential, so mastering the usage and blending of colors is a skill that pays off. Get a set of high-quality gel food coloring that will give you vivid colors without sacrificing the consistency of your frosting. Learn about color theory to make harmonious pairings, or try out monochromatic palettes for a more polished appearance. Gaining proficiency in color application requires a grasp of color intensity and how it interacts with the cookie surface. Practice color flooding and blending techniques to create seamless gradients and transitions in your designs.

With relative ease, cookies can be embellished with complex patterns and decorations using the multipurpose stenciling. Powdered sugar, cocoa powder, or colored icing can be applied with food-safe stencils to make intricate and elegant-looking embellishments. Beginners can accomplish remarkable effects with stenciling without requiring extensive freehand skills. It's a valuable tool in your cookie-decorating arsenal because it makes designs consistent and repeatable.

Accepting mistakes as opportunities for progress and adopting a growth attitude are critical components of developing confidence when decorating cookies. Recognize that imperfections exist in all cookies, and that's acceptable. Every decorated cookie is a learning tool, and your abilities will improve as you use them. Give your work to friends, family, or members of an online community. Positive reinforcement and constructive criticism aid in the learning process and increase self-assurance.

Try more difficult cookie decorating techniques as you become more comfortable with the fundamentals. Using wet-on-wet icing techniques, for example, you can overlay multiple icing colors while wet to create elaborate designs. This method produces beautiful and visually dramatic effects but takes some timing and accuracy. Try wet-on-wet techniques to broaden your decorating arsenal and give your cookies an added level of refinement.

Another way to boost your confidence and make eye-catching designs is to add texture to your cookies. Your biscuits will seem fanciful and artistic if you utilize techniques like brush embroidery, which involves creating tiny textures on flooded icing with a damp brush. Adding edible components, such as glitter or sanding sugar, improves the overall visual appeal and the tactile sensation. You may add individuality and character to your cookie designs by experimenting with various textures.

Taking part in themed cookie decorating projects is a fun and disciplined method to experiment with new techniques and gain confidence. Themed projects provide a concentrated way to learn and practice particular skills, whether holiday-themed cookies, seasonal snacks, or personalized crafts for special occasions. They offer you the chance to play around with numerous patterns, hues, and embellishments, showcasing your development and originality in a well-organized collection with a theme.

Enrolling in live or virtual cookie decorating workshops is an excellent opportunity to get advice, pointers, and inspiration from seasoned decorators. Numerous knowledgeable decorators provide tutorials on various topics related to cookie decorating, from simple methods to intricate designs. These courses frequently offer a welcoming environment where students can discuss their experiences, pose inquiries, and acknowledge their accomplishments. Gaining confidence and inspiration to keep improving your cookie decorating abilities might come from talking to other enthusiasts and learning from more experienced decorators.

Gaining self-assurance via creative expression and self-discovery is the journey of cookie decorating. It's about appreciating development, accepting the learning curve, and discovering the joy of edible design. Simple cookies may be turned into gorgeous, customized pieces of art by even inexperienced decorators with a bit of perseverance, practice, and openness to trying new methods. So grab a piping bag, roll up your sleeves, and get ready to explore the delectable world of cookie decorating while gaining self-assurance and letting your creativity run wild.

CHAPTER VI

Intermediate Decorating Skills

Advancing Your Cookie Decorating Skills

Cookie decorating is a fun and artistic culinary endeavor that turns simple baked goods into mouthwatering artworks. The ambition to develop one's abilities and produce more elaborate and aesthetically pleasing designs frequently takes the stage as decorators go beyond the fundamentals. The path to improving cookie decorating abilities is gratifying and full of opportunities, from learning sophisticated piping techniques to experimenting with unusual textures and adding minute embellishments.

A key component of developing cookie decorating abilities is proficiency with sophisticated piping methods. While novice decorators usually begin with simple pipe designs like dots and swirls, more experienced decorators can add complex patterns and textures to make their projects pop. Techniques that hint at sophistication and elegance include lace piping, which involves pipetting tiny lace-like patterns onto cookies. The ability to control the piping bag with a steady hand and practice makes all the difference for decorators who want to produce intricate and visually stunning designs.

Moreover, royal icing, the preferred decorator medium, becomes a flexible tool for individuals looking to improve their abilities. Wet-on-wet icing techniques create new opportunities, enabling decorators to develop dynamic and bright designs by layering different icing colors while still wet. The outcomes of this technique are visually arresting and demonstrate a degree of talent that goes beyond the fundamentals. Still, it does need exact timing and a deep understanding of how colors interact.

In the hands of skilled decorators, edible stencils have become an increasingly sophisticated tool. With accuracy, intricate patterns, intricate designs, and sophisticated pictures can be put into cookies, giving the final product a polished appearance. Advanced stenciling techniques may require layering many stencils or combining different colors to get a multi-dimensional image. Decorators can express their creativity in a regulated way with stencil work, creating memorable, elaborate designs.

For decorators who want to get more proficient, texture becomes crucial. Cookies gain depth and dimension from techniques like brush embroidery, which uses a damp brush to create fine textures over flooded icing. The end effect is a tactile sensation that improves the cookie's artistic quality and visual attractiveness. Expert decorators play around with various instruments and methods to produce textures that can be delicate and refined or striking and dramatic.

Advanced decorating is characterized by the use of edible materials in cookie designs. Tools for glamming up cookies include edible glitter, sanding sugar, and metallic dust. It is possible to use the placement of edible components to highlight specific characteristics or provide a central focus in the design. Expert decorators know how to use these components to balance richness and restraint, resulting in a visually pleasing and harmonious finished piece.

Another advanced method that decorators might experiment with is cookie layering, stacking many cookies to produce a three-dimensional effect. Using royal icing as a glue and various cookie sizes and shapes, decorators may create complex and visually striking cookie constructions. Using this method, decorators may create more imaginative food scenarios, characters, or whole narrative cookie frameworks.

Eating paint provides a canvas for true artistic expression for cookie decorators who want to push the envelope. Decorators can create personalized and hand-painted masterpieces by painting intricate motifs directly onto cookies using edible food colors as a medium. Using edible paint, decorators may bring their thoughts to life with precise brushstrokes and a steady hand. A world of possibilities for making one-of-a-kind, customized, and gallery-worthy cookie designs becomes available with edible painting.

As cookie decorators get more proficient, airbrushing becomes a potent method for giving biscuits depth and dimension. Realistic shading and smooth gradients can be achieved by applying a tiny mist of edible color using airbrushing. This method works very well for adding backgrounds, gradients, and other details that improve the cookie's overall appeal. Decorators with advanced skills use airbrushing to give their products a sophisticated and polished look.

Decorators can develop their abilities in an organized and motivating way by participating in themed or group projects. Whether working together on cookie projects with other decorators or pushing oneself with themed projects, these activities inspire decorators to venture outside their comfort zones and experiment with novel approaches. Decorators are frequently caused by themed projects to try out new ideas, colors, and styles, which helps them develop and broaden their skill set.

Attending lessons or workshops on advanced cookie decorating provides an easy way to improve your skills. Experienced decorators frequently impart their knowledge by solving typical problems, offering individualized advice, and sharing insights into cutting-edge approaches. Topics like complex stenciling, airbrushing techniques, and complicated piping may be covered in advanced levels. Because workshops are hands-on, decorators can practice under the supervision of an expert instructor and receive quick feedback on their skills.

Technology can be helpful for decorators who want to improve their abilities. Many resources are available for learning new skills, keeping up with industry trends, and interacting with a global community of decorators, including online lessons, forums, and social media platforms. Decorators can learn at their own pace and repeat lessons as needed, thanks to video tutorials that provide step-by-step instructions on complex techniques. Decorators can also share their work, look for inspiration, and get helpful criticism in the internet forum.

Developing one's cookie decorating abilities involves ongoing education, trial and error, and creative investigation. Refining one's trade brings decorators fulfillment, whether they are learning complex piping techniques, combining exquisite textures, or pushing the boundaries with edible painting. The realm of cookie decorating provides an endless canvas for artistic expression. As decorators develop their abilities, they produce aesthetically magnificent edible artwork and encourage others to take their sweet journeys of creative exploration and skill development.

Intermediate Techniques and Designs

With practice and exploration, cookie decorating becomes an increasingly satisfying and enjoyable art form. The intermediate level is essential for decorators as they go from fundamental skills to more complex approaches. Decorators can push their creative limits with intermediate techniques and designs, honing their craft while producing striking and technically excellent cookies.

Proficiency with sophisticated piping procedures is a crucial competency at the intermediate stage. Intermediate decorators can play with more intricate patterns and textures, but fundamental designs set the groundwork. Decorators can achieve smoother surfaces for elaborate designs by using techniques like flooding, which become second nature when done consistently and precisely. Various piping tips are used at this stage to produce features such as lace, filigree, and ruffles. Intermediate piping is known for its ability to control icing flow and create fine details, which enables decorators to elevate their cookie designs to a higher level.

The basic cookie decorating technique of stenciling expands to a new level at the intermediate level. Beyond simple patterns, decorators experiment with complex designs and build depth by stacking many stencils. The level of accuracy needed to align stencils and apply the appropriate quantity of edible media increases. Intermediate decorators can demonstrate their abilities to customize and enhance their cookie masterpieces by experimenting with specially designed stencils or adapting pre-existing designs.

In intermediate cookie decorating, texture is essential, and designers use sophisticated techniques to give their patterns more depth and appeal. Brush embroidery is a method that enables the insertion of lacy or flowery designs on flooded icing. It involves using a damp brush to produce delicate textures. The deft application of edible components, like edible glitter or sanding sugar, improves the cookies' overall appearance and tactile sensation. Intermediate decorators experiment with various tools, such as embossing tools and stippling brushes, to produce textured effects and broaden their toolkit.

As decorators get to the intermediate level, color theory becomes increasingly essential. It becomes crucial to comprehend color psychology, play around with color combinations, and design eye-catching palettes. Decorators learn to avoid common mistakes like color leaking by using gel food colors to achieve rich and consistent hues. Intermediate cookie decorating is characterized by the ability to produce ombre effects, gradients, and smooth color transitions, which elevate the final designs to a higher level.

At the intermediate level, wet-on-wet icing techniques are improved and expanded upon after being taught in the primary stages. To create visually dynamic designs, decorators experiment with stacking multiple colors while preserving the icing's fluidity. To investigate techniques to mix and integrate colors flawlessly, decorators must balance timing and precision using this technique. The intermediate stage demonstrates a higher degree of ability and artistry by enabling the creation of complex designs, such as flowers, marbling effects, or abstract patterns.

In intermediate cookie decorating, the use of edible materials as embellishments gets increasingly advanced. To improve their creations, decorators play around with the sizes and forms of edible pearls, dragees, and metallic components. To compliment their designs without overpowering them, decorators must carefully consider composition and balance while placing these pieces. Intermediate decorators transform their cookies into tiny culinary works of art using glitzy and luxurious embellishments.

Advanced piping suggestions turn into indispensable resources for intermediate decorators. Designers experiment using specialized tips, such as leaf or petal tips, to give their creations more depth and texture. With these specific tips, decorators may create cookies that resemble tiny works of edible art, complete with piped flowers, delicate borders, and detailed leaves. Intermediate cookie decorating gains a degree of intentionality and precision from the ability to select the appropriate tip for a particular design.

Three-dimensional design is made accessible to decorators through many cookie layers. Expert decorators experiment with stacking cookies of varying sizes and forms, binding them with royal icing. With this method, one can make delicious scenes, tiered decorations, or even sculptures out of cookies. As decorators hone their craft, they discover how to balance the stacked cookies' structural integrity and the overall design's aesthetic appeal, producing delicious artwork that will make an impact.

Themed or seasonal projects are a great source of inspiration for intermediate decorators. Crafting a batch of cookies for a noteworthy event or participating in a themed cooperative effort with fellow decorators offer a targeted arena for honing skills. Decorators must use their imaginations, try out novel methods, and convey their artistic vision within a predetermined framework when working on themed projects. This method pushes decorators' creative bounds and promotes growth, creating cookies that tell a compelling and eye-catching story.

Participating in cookie decorating forums and going to workshops at the intermediate level are great ways for decorators to hone their craft. Decorators can share their work, trade ideas, and get helpful criticism on these groups' platforms. Advanced techniques like dimensional piping, complex stenciling, and advanced airbrushing are frequently covered in intermediate workshops, which offer individualized teaching and practical advice. The progress and confidence of intermediate decorators are facilitated by the shared excitement and sense of kinship within these societies.

Social media and online platforms are crucial in the intermediate stage of cookie decorating. Decorators create a virtual place for inspiration and education by sharing their creations on websites like Pinterest, Instagram, and cookie decorating communities. Decorators can study at their own pace with the help of step-by-step instructions on advanced techniques provided by decorators in the form of video lessons. Online communities create a community among cookie decorating lovers by offering a global network for decorators to interact, exchange ideas, and celebrate their accomplishments.

Decorators establish their unique style as they move through the intermediate level. Experimentation with different methods, materials, and styles aids in developing a distinct artistic voice. Intermediate decorators start to hone and identify their style, whether it's a penchant for detailed piping, a love of vivid and intense colors, or a talent for building three-dimensional structures. At this point, they have moved from studying and practicing to creating a unique style that makes them stand out in the cookie-decorating community.

To sum up, the intermediate period of cookie decorating is crucial and fascinating since it allows decorators to hone their abilities, try cutting-edge methods, and develop their unique artistic style. During this stage, decorators discover a world of creative possibilities by exploring textures, colors, and three-dimensional designs and learning sophisticated piping and stenciling techniques. Gaining more expertise in cookie decorating is a journey that combines education with artistic discovery, giving decorators the ability and self-assurance to turn straightforward cookies into elaborate, visually attractive edible works of art.

Troubleshooting Tips for Intermediate Challenges

As cookie decorators progress through the intermediate levels, they frequently encounter fresh difficulties due to honing their craft to the limit. Overcoming obstacles like mastering complex plumbing procedures and handling the intricacies of multi-layered designs calls for a blend of expertise, problem-solving abilities, and imagination. This essay will discuss some typical intermediate decorating problems and offer solutions to assist decorators in getting past these roadblocks and moving forward in their quest to become experts in edible design.

Reaching a uniform icing consistency is a common issue in intermediate cookie decorating. Intermediate decorators play around with different icing consistencies, such as flooding for background smoothness and stiff icing for fine details. However, it might be challenging to get the ideal consistency. It might be challenging to pipe complex designs if the icing is too thick. If it is too thin, it can flood out of control and lose definition. The secret to conquering this obstacle is observation and practice. Decorators should know how their icing flows and gradually change the consistency to get the desired effects. Furthermore, consistency guidelines can be helpful as a point of reference. One such guideline is the "10-second rule" for flooding icing.

A further intermediate task is to become proficient in advanced piping methods. While decorators at this level have probably mastered the fundamentals of piping, more expertise is needed to move on to more complex patterns like lacework or delicate filigree—one frequent problem when plumbing is keeping the pressure constant. Only some lines or details might result from consistent pressure. Decorators should practice applying pressure to the piping bag with a steady hand to troubleshoot this. Precision can be attained by gradually increasing pressure for thicker lines and decreasing it for minor details. Advanced piping methods can also be mastered by experimenting with various pipe tips and learning about their distinctive qualities.

In the middle stages, stenciling becomes more intricate, but decorators could run into issues with bleed-through colors or jagged patterns. This problem typically occurs when the stencil is not pushed firmly against the cookie or when the icing underneath the stencil is excessively wet. Decorators should ensure the icing base layer is completely set before putting on the stencil to prevent bleeding. Furthermore, color bleed can be avoided by carefully slapping the stencil onto the cookie and securing it in place. Sharper and better-defined stenciled designs can also be achieved by experimenting with the type of stencil and the quantity of edible medium utilized.

As decorators explore more complex techniques like brush embroidery or incorporating edible items as ornaments, texture issues arise. Sticking to the ideal texture balance might be challenging without detracting from the overall composition. Decorators should learn how to apply the proper amount of pressure while brushing embroidery and comprehend the relationship between a damp brush and flooding icing. Excessive pressure can distort the pattern, while insufficient pressure can not produce the intended texture. Decorators should consider each addition's physical and visual effects when adding edible materials. By experimenting with various textures and positions, decorators might discover the ideal point when the design is enhanced without overpowering.

In the intermediate stages, color management becomes a more complex problem, mainly when working on intricate designs with various hues and gradients. It can be challenging to maintain color intensity and make smooth transitions. One frequent situation is color bleeding when neighboring colors blend and lose the design's clarity. Decorators should ensure that every color layer is completely set before moving on to the next to address the issue. This can entail using a fan or giving each layer more time to dry. Additionally, decorators can accomplish seamless color transitions by practicing color blending techniques like feathering or wet-on-wet gradients.

Although wet-on-wet icing techniques give designs a dynamic touch, they also provide a unique set of difficulties for intermediate decorators. Timing is essential when trying to achieve effects like marbling or layered graphics. Waiting too long between layers is a common problem that results in icing that is too dry to merge well. Decorators should experiment with tiny test cookies to find the best timing for their particular icing consistency and ambient circumstances to troubleshoot this. Practical work and prepping all colors needed are critical components of successful wet-on-wet techniques.

Integrating numerous cookie layers presents issues with cohesive design and structural stability. If stacked cookies are not put together correctly, they may move or collapse. When using royal icing as an adhesive, decorators should ensure that the thickness is just right—not too thick to give the impression of mass. Stability can be increased by carefully positioning supporting components inside the construction, such as extra icing or dowels. While creating aesthetically pleasing three-dimensional effects, decorators can learn about the mechanics of structural integrity by experimenting with different cookie shapes and sizes in a layered design.

While themed or collaborative initiatives offer a focused and motivating approach, they can present obstacles in sustaining a consistent theme among numerous cookies. Maintaining consistency in design elements, color palettes, and overall aesthetics can be difficult when working on a broader scale. Decorators should prepare their designs ahead of time to provide a consistent color scheme and theme to troubleshoot this for every design piece; making a prototype or drawing aids in preserving consistency throughout the project. Working with other decorators can also yield insightful comments and ideas for improving and coordinating specific designs within the theme.

Participating in cookie decorating forums and workshops is difficult, particularly when turning digital inspiration into real-world masterpieces. It could be difficult for decorators to duplicate particular methods or reach the same degree of accuracy as expert decorators. Decorators should use online workshops and tutorials as educational opportunities rather than strict guidelines to overcome this difficulty. Decorators can adjust and hone their skills by trying out each technique on tiny test cookies, which makes learning more flexible and pleasurable.

Decorators must adopt a philosophy of constant improvement as they work through these intermediate hurdles.

Troubleshooting Tips for Intermediate Challenges

By pushing the limits of their abilities, decorators who advance into the intermediate levels of cookie decorating face a new set of difficulties. One frequently needs a blend of expertise, problem-solving skills, and inventiveness to overcome these obstacles. This essay will discuss some typical intermediate decorating problems and offer solutions to assist decorators in getting beyond these obstacles and moving forward in their quest to become experts in edible design.

A common problem for intermediate decorators is getting the consistency of the icing right. Getting the consistency right can be challenging as decorators experiment with different icing consistencies, such as flooding for smooth backgrounds and stiff icing for detailed features. It might be challenging to pipe complex designs if the icing is too thick. If it is too thin, it can flood out of control and lose definition. The secret to conquering this obstacle is observation and practice. Decorators should know how their icing flows and
gradually change the consistency to get the desired effects. Furthermore, consistency guidelines can be helpful as a point of reference. One such guideline is the "10-second rule" for flooding icing.

Another obstacle for intermediate decorators is using sophisticated piping techniques. While decorators at this level have probably mastered the fundamentals of piping, more expertise is needed to move on to more complex patterns like lacework or delicate filigree—one frequent problem when plumbing is keeping the pressure constant. Only some lines or details might result from consistent pressure. Decorators should practice applying pressure to the piping bag with a steady hand to troubleshoot this. Precision can be attained by gradually increasing pressure for thicker lines and decreasing it for minor details. Advanced piping methods can also be mastered by experimenting with various pipe tips and learning about their distinctive qualities.

In the middle stages, stenciling becomes more intricate, but decorators could run into issues with bleed-through colors or jagged patterns. This problem typically occurs when the stencil is not pushed firmly against the cookie or when the icing underneath the stencil is excessively wet. Decorators should ensure the icing base layer is completely set before putting on the stencil to prevent bleeding. Furthermore, color bleed can be avoided by carefully slapping the stencil onto the cookie and securing it in place. Sharper and better-defined stenciled designs can also be achieved by experimenting with the type of stencil and the quantity of edible medium utilized.

As decorators explore more complex techniques like brush embroidery or incorporating edible items as ornaments, texture issues arise. Sticking to the ideal texture balance might be challenging without detracting from the overall composition. Decorators should learn how to apply the proper amount of pressure while brushing embroidery and comprehend the relationship between a damp brush and flooding icing. Excessive pressure can distort the pattern, while insufficient pressure can not produce the intended texture. Decorators should consider each addition's physical and visual effects when adding edible materials. By experimenting with various textures and positions, decorators might discover the ideal point when the design is enhanced without overpowering.

In the intermediate stages, color management becomes a more complex problem, mainly when working on intricate designs with various hues and gradients. It can be challenging to maintain color intensity and make smooth transitions. One frequent situation is color bleeding when neighboring colors blend and lose the design's clarity. Decorators should ensure that every color layer is completely set before moving on to the next to address the issue. This can entail using a fan or giving each layer more time to dry. Additionally, decorators can accomplish seamless color transitions by practicing color blending techniques like feathering or wet-on-wet gradients.

Although wet-on-wet icing techniques give designs a dynamic touch, they also provide a unique set of difficulties for intermediate decorators. Timing is essential when trying to achieve effects like marbling or layered graphics. Waiting too long between layers is a common problem that results in icing that is too dry to merge well. Decorators should experiment with tiny test cookies to find the best timing for their particular icing consistency and ambient circumstances to troubleshoot this. Practical work and prepping all colors needed are critical components of successful wet-on-wet techniques.

Integrating numerous cookie layers presents issues with cohesive design and structural stability. If stacked cookies are not put together correctly, they may move or collapse. When using royal icing as an adhesive, decorators should ensure that the thickness is just right—not too thick to give the impression of mass. Stability can be increased by carefully positioning supporting components inside the construction, such as extra icing or dowels. While creating aesthetically pleasing three-dimensional effects, decorators can learn about the mechanics of structural integrity by experimenting with different cookie shapes and sizes in a layered design.

While themed or collaborative initiatives offer a focused and motivating approach, they can present obstacles in sustaining a consistent theme among numerous cookies. Maintaining consistency in design elements, color palettes, and overall aesthetics can be difficult when working on a broader scale. Decorators should prepare their designs ahead of time to provide a consistent color scheme and theme to troubleshoot this for every design piece; making a prototype or drawing aids in preserving consistency throughout the project. Working with other decorators can also yield insightful comments and ideas for improving and coordinating specific designs within the theme.

Participating in cookie decorating forums and workshops is difficult, particularly when turning digital inspiration into real-world masterpieces. It could be difficult for decorators to duplicate particular methods or reach the same degree of accuracy as expert decorators. Decorators should use online workshops and tutorials as educational opportunities rather than strict guidelines to overcome this difficulty. Decorators can adjust and hone their skills by trying out each technique on tiny test cookies, which makes learning more flexible and pleasurable.

Decorators must adopt a philosophy of ongoing learning and development as they negotiate these intermediate hurdles. Every obstacle offers a chance for skill development and improvement. A decorator's toolkit should include troubleshooting ideas and strategies as they aid in overcoming challenges and gaining a deeper comprehension of the craft of cookie decorating. Intermediate decorators can overcome obstacles and create cookies that exhibit their technical mastery and artistic flair in culinary design if they have the patience, practice, and openness to try new things.

CHAPTER VII

Expert-Level Cookie Decorating

Mastering the Art of Elaborate Cookie Designs

Cookie decorating is an artistic and culinary endeavor, allowing people to express their creativity and turn essential baked items into elaborate, delicious works of art. The urge to become proficient in intricate cookie designs motivates decorators' artistic development as they move from fundamental methods to more sophisticated abilities. Technical skills, creative insight, and a profound respect for the profession are all necessary for this expertise. This essay delves into the

various facets of proficiency in intricate cookie designs, encompassing the fundamental abilities and the subtle methods that transform cookies into delectable artworks.

A strong foundation in the fundamentals of cookie decorating is essential to achieving intricate cookie patterns. Decorators must practice consistently rolling out uniform cookie dough, baking cookies to perfection, and making royal icing before tackling more complex designs. These fundamental abilities act as the blank canvas on which intricate patterns are painted. The ability to grasp these foundational concepts guarantees a solid foundation for the progressively complicated methods and specifics that come next.

The foundation of intricate cookie patterns is piping abilities; becoming proficient is a big step in a decorator's career. In addition to skill in crafting elaborate designs, advanced piping calls for a deep comprehension of the interactions between various piping tips and icing consistencies. Decorators must learn how to manage the icing flow, apply steady pressure to the piping bag, and understand the subtle differences between tips. Decorators who have mastered the art of intricate cookie designs are known for
executing complex patterns with elegance, from delicate lacework to intricate floral motifs.

The decorator's preferred material, royal icing, becomes a flexible instrument for ambitious people who want to create intricate designs. Getting the ideal consistency for outlining, flooding, and detailing is crucial. The nuances of dealing with various consistencies, such as firm icing for fine details and thin icing for smooth flooding, must be understood by decorators. To ensure that the icing improves rather than detracts from the overall design, royal icing mastery requires technical ability and an intuitive grasp of how the icing performs under various conditions.

Complex cookie designs heavily rely on color theory. Understanding the psychology of color, experimenting with color combinations, and creating brilliant yet harmonious palettes are all part of mastering the art of color. Decorators must be proficient with gel food coloring to achieve exact hues without sacrificing the icing's consistency. The key to taking cookie decorating to a more intricate and creative level is mastering color application, whether for subtle and refined color schemes or significant and dramatic motifs.

Wet-on-wet icing techniques give sophisticated designs an extra layer of complexity, enabling decorators to produce visually dynamic effects, complicated patterns, and seamless transitions. Learning wet-on-wet techniques requires a thorough understanding of color interaction, blending, and exact timing while layering different colors. The viscosity of the icing must be experimented with, and decorators must learn how to blend colors to create gradients, marbled effects, and multi-dimensional designs. A careful balance between
precision and patience is needed for this method.

Stenciling is standard in elaborate cookie designs to add detailed patterns and textures. Stenciling is a skill that requires careful stencil creation or selection, precise cookie placement, and deft application of edible material. Decorators must solve problems like bleed colors or crooked patterns to ensure the stenciled pieces work well together. Stenciling demonstrates a decorator's attention to detail and accuracy in executing complicated designs.

The texture becomes essential when it comes to mastering intricate cookie designs. The designs get depth and character from techniques like brush embroidery, which uses a damp brush to create fine textures over flooded icing. The ability to add delicate or striking textures that accentuate the cookies' visual appeal without drawing attention away from the arrangement is a talent that decorators must master.
The deft use of edible components, such as metallic dust or sanding sugar, enhances the tactile and visual experience even more, resulting in aesthetically pleasing and pleasurable cookies.
By adding layers to intricate cookie designs, decorators can venture into the world of three-dimensional

masterpieces. Combining stacked or layered cookies can create elaborate structures, scenarios, or themed designs. Understanding the structural integrity of cookies, utilizing royal icing as a dependable glue, and experimenting with various shapes and sizes to produce eye-catching results are all necessary for mastering this method. In multi-layered designs, decorators must balance the aesthetic vision and the pragmatic concerns of coherence and stability.

Edible painting gives intricate cookie designs a painterly quality that enables decorators to craft personalized, hand-painted works of art. Acquiring proficiency in this method requires the artistic ability to paint intricate details and knowledge of edible food coloring as a medium. To get the necessary effects, decorators must experiment with brush techniques, color blending, and shading. Edible painting gives decorators new ways to express themselves and add distinctive artistic elements to their creations.

Expert airbrushing methods are invaluable for decorators who want to create intricate designs. Applying a thin mist of edible color with an airbrush creates realistic shading, detailed backgrounds, and smooth gradients. To create visually dynamic effects, a creative eye and technical ability with the airbrush tool are required for airbrushing mastery. To get the correct detail in their designs, decorators must experiment with different masks, airbrushing pressures, and templates.

Decorators can demonstrate their proficiency with complex cookie designs by participating in themed or group initiatives. Themed projects inspire decorators to explore their creativity, whether making a batch of cookies for a particular event or working together on a project with other decorators. The capacity of a decorator to bring a unified concept to life is demonstrated by their ability to smoothly blend intricate designs, textures, and techniques within a themed project.

For cookie decorators looking to hone their craft, taking advanced cookie decorating workshops or classes is a great option. Experienced decorators frequently teach advanced skills like precise piping, detailed stenciling, and sophisticated airbrushing in their workshops. Because these seminars are hands-on, decorators can get quick feedback, solve problems in real-time, and hone their skills under the supervision of a skilled instructor. Participant camaraderie is another benefit of workshops; they create a community of decorators passionate about creating intricate cookie patterns.

Technology utilization, mainly social media and online platforms, become useful for decorators skilled in creating complex designs. Decorators can learn at their own pace and review lessons as needed with the help of video tutorials with seasoned decorators who provide step-by-step instructions on complex methods. Online communities offer decorators a global network to interact, exchange ideas, and celebrate their intricate works of art. Social networking sites transform into online galleries where decorators may share their expertise, motivate others, and get input from a wide range of users.

As cookie decorators advance to become experts in intricate designs, they acquire a unique style that distinguishes their works. Technical mastery, artistic expression, and a personal touch create this unique look. Cookie decorators start to carve out a name for themselves in the industry, whether through a penchant for complex three-dimensional constructions, a mastery of vivid color palettes, or a fondness for exquisite piping. The decorator's ability, perseverance, and inventiveness have peaked, demonstrating their commitment to creating intricate cookie designs.

Professional Tips and Tricks

In the ever-changing world of the modern professional, people are always looking for new methods to succeed and improve their performance. A person's career trajectory can be significantly impacted by various professional tips and tricks, ranging from developing good communication skills to becoming proficient in time management. This essay explores crucial tactics people can use to further their career goals.

Any working success mainly depends on communication, so developing strong communication skills is a critical professional tip. Establishing and maintaining successful interpersonal connections can be facilitated by the capacity to listen intently, communicate ideas clearly, and modify communication techniques to suit a variety of audiences. Professionals with solid communication skills are frequently advantaged in group tasks, dealing with clients, or taking on leadership positions. Awareness of non-verbal clues like body language and facial expressions can also help increase communication effectiveness.

Another essential component of professional development is strategic networking. Developing a solid professional network can lead to new opportunities, offer insightful information, and even create mentorship opportunities. Making sincere connections with peers, coworkers, and business executives is the essence of networking, which extends beyond simply going to events. By showcasing their skills and keeping up with industry developments, people can grow their professional network using sites like LinkedIn.

Adopting a proactive stance toward ongoing education is a precious suggestion in the constantly changing field of work. Since industries and technology are constantly evolving, people who commit to lifelong learning position themselves as invaluable resources for their companies. Learning new abilities through seminars, online courses, or formal education shows flexibility and a commitment to professional development.

Time management is a constant struggle on the job, and professionals frequently have to juggle several responsibilities simultaneously. Setting reasonable deadlines, prioritizing work, and using productivity tools can all significantly increase productivity. For example, the Pomodoro Technique maximizes productivity by encouraging people to work in focused periods with brief breaks. Effective time management improves team performance as a whole in addition to improving individual performance.

Emotional intelligence is increasingly recognized as a pivotal skill in the workplace. Professionals skilled in managing their own emotions and those of others cultivate productive work environments and harmoniously resolve conflicts. Proficiency in interpersonal skills, self-control, empathy, and self-awareness are all integral to developing emotional intelligence. Professionals who nurture their emotional intelligence are better equipped to navigate complex workplace dynamics with poise, make informed decisions, and build robust relationships with their colleagues, contributing to a harmonious and efficient work environment.

Maintaining a robust online presence in the digital era cannot be overstated. Professionals should actively curate their brands to ensure their online profiles accurately reflect their skills, achievements, and career aspirations. Enhancing one's online presence can be achieved by regularly updating their LinkedIn profile, engaging in industry discussions on social media, and showcasing their expertise through blog posts or articles. A robust digital presence increases one's visibility in the industry and bolsters professional credibility, making it a key component of career advancement in the digital age.

Strong negotiating abilities, such as wage negotiations and project collaboration, are essential in work-related situations. Professionals are more likely to succeed when they can express their demands effectively, comprehend the interests of others, and come up with win-win solutions. Effective negotiating strategies require preparation; knowing the pertinent data, foreseeing possible objections, and remaining flexible throughout the process are all necessary for success.

Many professionals struggle to find a balance between their personal and professional lives. In today's fast-paced work environments, burnout is a genuine worry. To achieve long-term success, people need to emphasize self-care. Essential components of a healthy work-life balance include establishing limits, taking breaks, and identifying the warning signs of burnout. Employers value employees who put their well-being first more and more since doing so increases output and job happiness.

To sum up, achieving professional success requires various abilities, including time management, emotional intelligence, intelligent networking, effective communication, solid online presence, negotiation, and a positive work-life balance. These career-boosting advice and techniques aren't stand-alone acts; instead, they're linked tactics that, when used in concert, can help people achieve professional success. Sustaining success requires adjusting and incorporating these recommendations into one's approach, which is more
important as the professional scene changes.

Showcasing Your Expertise

The ability to adequately demonstrate one's expertise is a critical talent that can considerably influence one's career trajectory in the competitive world of today's professional landscape. Professionals must go beyond being competent in their professions as sectors change and grow more interconnected; to stand out in the competitive marketplace, they must actively demonstrate their skills and knowledge. This essay examines a range of tactics and approaches that people can use to show their expertise, such as building a robust online presence and participating in industry networks.

Developing a solid online presence is one of the most effective strategies for demonstrating knowledge in the digital era. Professionals can showcase their accomplishments and build their brand on LinkedIn, Twitter, and professional blogs. A polished LinkedIn profile functions as an online CV, enabling people to highlight their background, qualifications, and references. Engaging in active participation in industry discussions on social media sites such as Twitter showcases one's expertise and establishes oneself as an authority in their profession. Furthermore, keeping up a professional blog or writing for trade journals can build credibility and offer a forum for in-depth discussion of one's expertise.

Demonstrating knowledge is being current on industry trends and participating in ongoing learning. Professionals who commit to continuing education show that they are committed to remaining current in their industry. This could entail taking online classes, attending workshops, or getting advanced degrees. Keeping up with the most recent advancements in the field broadens one's expertise and establishes one as a knowledgeable, forward-thinking professional. Furthermore, the capacity to apply fresh perspectives to actual problems demonstrates a flexible and dynamic approach to problem-solving.
Another way for professionals to demonstrate their competence is through active involvement in industry events and professional associations. Acquiring membership in pertinent organizations grants one access to a community of like-minded people and chances to add to the body of knowledge on the subject. One can establish oneself as an authority on a topic by giving conference talks, participating in panel discussions, or organizing workshops. These activities also allow one to interact directly with colleagues and possible partners. Participating in professional societies also helps one get access to leadership positions, which enhances one's reputation as an authority in the field.

Developing a solid portfolio is a concrete method to demonstrate one's ability, especially in technical and artistic disciplines. A well-curated portfolio visualizes an individual's ability, whether achieved through various projects, case studies, or published works. It makes it possible for prospective clients, employers, or partners to evaluate the caliber of the professional's work and the breadth of their skill set. Maintaining a current and accurate representation of knowledge requires regularly updating and improving the portfolio.

In the academic domain, presenting findings at conferences and publishing research papers in respected publications are established means of demonstrating knowledge. These contributions broaden the field's collective understanding and solidify the author's reputation in academic circles. One's status as an expert in a given field is further validated by working with other scholars and actively engaging in peer review procedures.

One of the main components of demonstrating competence is the skill of efficient communication. Experts who simplify complex concepts into exciting and approachable information will have a higher chance of drawing in readers. This calls for understanding the wants and preferences of the audience in addition to communicating well both verbally and in writing. Professional exposure can be significantly increased by sharing expertise in an approachable way, whether talking with clients, peers, or the general public.

Using social proof to your advantage is another way to demonstrate your competence. Strong affirmations of one's expertise come from referrals, testimonials, and endorsements from clients, colleagues, or business titans. Beyond self-promotion, actively seeking and displaying good feedback on professional platforms or personal websites adds legitimacy. Building solid professional connections can also result in natural recommendations, creating a positive feedback loop highlighting knowledge.

Professional communities' collaboration and knowledge-sharing facilitate expertise display in a cooperative setting. Engaging in active participation in discussion groups, online forums, and peer mentorship within the industry showcases one's knowledge and fosters professional community development. Professionals exhibit generosity by contributing their ideas, best practices, and lessons gained to the communal knowledge pool openly and transparently.

Multimedia formats are a lively way to present your knowledge. Professionals can share their expertise through alternate media such as webinars, video material, and podcasts. These styles let people show their personalities and communication abilities while accommodating various learning preferences. A podcast series or webinar on industry-specific subjects might draw in a larger audience and position the host as an authority in the sector.

In summary, exhibiting knowledge is a complex process requiring a planned and proactive approach. Professionals have a wide range of tools, from actively participating in continuous learning and using multimedia formats to building a solid web presence and joining professional associations. The secret is to adopt a complete plan combining these methods to produce an extensive expert narrative that appeals to the target market. Demonstrating competence is a skill and a strategic necessity for career advancement in an era where success is often equated with professional exposure.

CHAPTER VIII

Holiday and Seasonal Cookie Decorating

Special Techniques for Festive Holidays

We have a particular place in our hearts for the holiday season, characterized by happiness, coziness, and a spirit of celebration. Holidays, whether associated with Christmas, Hanukkah, Diwali, Eid, or another culture, unite people and promote common customs. Looking for original ways to enhance these special moments as we navigate the celebrations is normal. This paper investigates unique methods for joyous occasions, exploring imaginative strategies to improve festivity.

The art of gift-giving is one of the enduring customs observed throughout joyous occasions. However, a unique method entails offering experiences rather than just transferring material goods. This could include spa days, weekend vacations, concert tickets, and cooking workshops. Experience-based presents foster enduring memories and underscore the value of cherished times over tangible belongings. The personal touch added by the carefully chosen experiences based on the recipient's preferences heightens the significance of the holiday celebration.

Adding ethnic rituals and customs to festivities is a great way to give them more depth and authenticity. These customs can strengthen a person's sense of kinship with their ancestry and have deep cultural or religious significance. These rituals create a rich tapestry of customs passed down over the years, including lighting candles during Hanukkah, decorating the Christmas tree, and creating colorful rangoli designs for Diwali. A deeper appreciation for the holiday season can result from accepting and comprehending these rituals.

Throughout all cultures, celebratory celebrations revolve around culinary delicacies. Instead of following the formulas, a unique method is experimenting with fusion cuisine, combining regional specialties with international tastes in classic holiday dishes. This represents the variety of contemporary celebrations and infuses the eating experience with a surprise aspect. For example, creating a wonderful fusion feast that adds a fresh twist to well-known customs might be achieved by integrating novel products or infusing spices from diverse cuisines into classic holiday recipes.

Storytelling becomes a magical skill during the Christmas season. Whether a theatrical production or a bespoke family novel, crafting an exceptional storyline gives festivities a unique and unforgettable touch. Using this method, a compelling story is created by fusing personal tales, cultural relevance, and the history of family customs. Families and communities can transmit their distinct stories to future generations through storytelling, fostering a sense of continuity and intergenerational connection.

Handcrafted decorations are a unique method that fosters creativity and camaraderie while adding a personal touch to the holiday atmosphere. Whether it's homemade garlands, wreaths, or ornaments, decorating becomes a joyful pastime in and of itself. Crafting is an excellent way for people to show their creativity, involve family members in a project, and make a celebration more ecologically friendly and sustainable.

Taking up the giving mentality is a unique approach that enhances the happiness of the festive seasons. Rather than concentrating only on private celebrations, people might commit their time and resources to humanitarian endeavors. This may be setting up donation drives, community service initiatives, or volunteering at nearby shelters. Kindness captures the season's essence, develops empathy, and ties people to the community. During the frequently chaotic holiday season, a unique method that encourages serenity and introspection is the integration of mindfulness activities. Amidst the celebrations, people might find moments of peace by practicing yoga, meditation, or mindful breathing techniques. This method promotes a greater awareness of the relationships between people and their surroundings and a better appreciation for the present. By incorporating mindfulness into holiday festivities, happy exuberance and inner tranquility can coexist harmoniously.

Photographically capturing the spirit of the holidays is a unique method that will help you cherish those memories for years. Investing in professional or semi-professional photography sessions might improve the visual documentation of festivities, as opposed to depending only on smartphone photos. Whether it's a professionally organized album, a family portrait, or unposed shots of the festivities getting ready, the visual narrative created by images becomes a lasting memento that can be viewed again and passed down through the years.

Live music acts or carefully selected playlists are essential in establishing the celebratory atmosphere. Examining various musical traditions and bringing in a range of genres to add to the festive mood is a unique approach. From classic Christmas songs to world rhythms, music has an unmatched ability to arouse feelings and heighten the joyous atmosphere. An inclusive and lively celebration can be created by organizing live musical performances or working together to produce playlists that highlight a variety of cultural influences.

Using technology provides a unique way to stay in touch with loved ones, especially during the holidays when families and friends live apart. With the help of live streaming, video conversations, and virtual celebrations, people can spread the holiday cheer to friends who might be far away. In addition to bridging the gap between loved ones who live far away, integrating technology into festivities creates the possibility of imaginative and engaging virtual get-togethers like online gaming, virtual gift exchanges, and collaborative cooking sessions.

To summarize, joyful occasions provide a blank canvas for expression, kinship, and joy. The unique approaches discussed in this essay provide people with various methods to improve and customize their holiday celebrations, from fusion food and mindful practices to experiential gift-giving and cultural customs. These strategies encourage us to embrace the depth of customs, cultivate deep connections, and bring joy, creativity, and beloved memories into the celebrations—moments that will be remembered for years.

Seasonal Cookie Decorating Ideas

A few activities better capture the spirit of celebration than cookie decorating, bringing joy to the house's heart for the holidays. Cookie decorating is a long-standing custom that crosses ethnic barriers and is a fun way for people to spend quality time together and showcase their culinary creativity. This essay looks at various seasonal cookie decorating ideas to provide ideas for people who want to make their kitchens into festive workshops and turn regular cookies into delectable works of art.

The festive emblems of winter and the holidays are a classic and widely loved theme for seasonal cookie decorating. These timeless themes, which range from snowflakes and snowmen to Christmas trees and gingerbread houses, offer a blank canvas to express creativity. These symbols can be given life by frosting in various shades, allowing decorators to experiment with varied textures, colors, and patterns. These designs are an excellent place for cookie decorators of all experience levels to start because of their familiarity and simplicity, which leave room for creativity.

Decorating cookies can uniquely express cultural and familial customs, especially for those who want a more customized touch. People can get ideas from particular colors and symbols connected to their ancestry, depending on the occasion. For Diwali, one may create elaborate henna designs with colorful royal icing, and for Hanukkah, one could develop cookies shaped like stars or dreidels with accents of blue and silver. Decorators respect their heritage while crafting cookies that capture the essence of their celebrations by incorporating cultural themes into their designs.

Seasonal cookie decorators might get ideas from the beauty of nature by looking at the winter scenery. With various icing techniques, cookies can be delicately decorated to resemble delicate snow-covered landscapes, frost-kissed branches, and forest creatures. To create the illusion of snow, royal icing can be piped with skill, and edible metallic accents can bring a bit of winter wonder to the scene. Shapes of woodland animals, like owls or deer, can be beautifully adorned to create an enchanting atmosphere and bring the outside within the cozy kitchen.

Using accents in jewel tones and metallics is a new trend in holiday cookie decorating. Cookies may be transformed into glittering edible artwork by adding metallic icing, edible dust in gold and silver, and shimmering sprinkles. These opulent accents can be used on various designs, such as sophisticated monograms or geometric patterns, to give the festive table a glamorous touch. These cookies are a visually arresting addition to any celebration because light interacts with metallic surfaces to create a cheery glow. Seasonal cookie decorating can feel joy when it incorporates whimsical and playful themes. These cookies are meant to make you smile and chuckle, whether based on nostalgic childhood scenes or well-known holiday characters. With the help of vivid colors and inventive piping techniques, cookies can be decorated to resemble Santa Claus, elves, reindeer, and even characters from beloved Christmas movies. Decorators can experiment with 3D cookie designs for a fun twist. By stacking smaller cookies, they can make delicious sculptures that serve as festive centerpieces.

You are not limited to using typical holiday colors when decorating cookies. Trying out novel color schemes is a daring and contemporary strategy. Holiday cookies can seem sleek and modern with jewel tones, pastel colors, or even monochromatic designs. Decorators can now adapt their cookies to specific themes, house decor, or personal tastes, thanks to this deviation from the traditional red and green. The end product is an eye-catching display of cookies that add flair and distinction to any dessert table.

Adding edible textures and patterns is a creative take on seasonal cookie decorating. Cookies may become tiny works of art using techniques like edible lace, marbled fondant, and embossed fondant to give them a tactile quality. The fine details produced using these techniques give the overall design more depth and refinement. For a contemporary marble impression or a classic lace look, experimenting with textures adds a creative element that turns biscuits into eye-catching delights.

Decorators in the spirit of inclusion and diversity can welcome the idea of tailoring cookies to accommodate different dietary needs. It's now feasible to make delectable cookies that are gluten-free, vegan, or allergy-friendly, thanks to the development of substitute ingredients and baking techniques. This careful planning guarantees that everyone may enjoy delicious goodies and cookie-decorating fun regardless of dietary limitations. It's a chance to make everyone feel cozy and included by spreading the joy of the holidays.
Turning seasonal cookie baking into a festive cookie decorating party makes it a fascinating and involved activity. A cookie decorating party with friends and family adds a social component to the Christmas planning process and enables participants to exchange

advice, ideas, and creative solutions. Offering a range of cookie forms, hues, and decorating supplies promotes a team environment where everyone may add to the assortment of cookies. Collaborative crafting creates a delightful atmosphere and provides everyone with delectable mementos to cherish.

To sum up, decorating seasonal cookies is a fun and adaptable custom that lets people showcase their artistic side while bringing cheer to others. The options are endless, whether one works with textures, incorporates cultural themes, studies current trends, or takes inspiration from iconic icons. This edible art form's beauty is in its capacity to unite people, generate enduring memories, and infuse the holiday season with a hint of sweetness. The magic of seasonal cookie decorating happens as kitchens become joyful workshops and regular cookies become exceptional expressions of celebration

Creating Memorable Cookies for Every Occasion

Few foods provide the same happiness and nostalgia as a carefully prepared, beautifully adorned cookie. With their infinite range of tastes, forms, and patterns, cookies have come to be associated with festivities and serve as a delightful way to commemorate life's significant occasions. This essay explores the various methods, ideas, and sources of inspiration that turn these delicious delicacies into eatable manifestations of happiness and celebration. It also dives into the art of crafting unique cookies for any occasion.

Learning the art of flavor pairing is one of the essential components of making cookies that people will remember. Although traditional cookie varieties like chocolate chip or sugar cookies are still beloved by many, there is a wide variety of cookie flavors to try. The flavor profile can be changed to fit the occasion, ranging from rich triple chocolate chunk cookies to shortbread with a hint of citrus. Use flowery accents like lavender or rosewater for spring events and warm spices like cinnamon, nutmeg, and spiced pumpkin for fall get-togethers. Bakers can create memorable cookies by choosing flavors that complement the theme or season.

Cookie designs and shapes are essential in determining the mood of certain events. The possibilities are as varied as the holidays, ranging from elaborately decorated snowflakes for winter festivities to heart-shaped sweets for Valentine's Day. Various shaped and sized cookie cutters serve as the basis for artistic expression. For birthdays, try making cookies that match the honoree's age or include shapes associated with their hobbies. Adorable onesies or baby booties can be used as decorations for baby showers, while diploma and cap shapes can be used in graduation sweets. Because cookie shapes are so versatile, countless personalization options are available to celebrate every occasion with a unique and eye-catching treat.
Bakers can customize their creations to fit particular occasions, interests, or hobbies by using themed cookie decorating, which opens up a world of creative possibilities. For those who love sports, cookie designs like basketballs, soccer balls, or jerseys can liven up game day festivities. Elegant and romantic designs, such as elaborately piped lace patterns or personalized monogram cookies, are perfect for weddings. Animal-shaped cookies or fictional characters from a child's favorite books can add whimsy to the dessert table for a

birthday celebration. The secret is to make the visual experience pleasant and well-coordinated by coordinating the cookie theme with the event's mood.

The presentation of cookies has become a crucial component of making delicacies that people will remember in the age of social media and visually stimulating content. Cookie styling is an art form that requires meticulous attention to color, texture, and placement. Decorators can use a color scheme that goes well with the event for a unified effect. A sophisticated touch can be added with edible metallic decorations, shimmering dust, or flowers. The visual effect is increased when cookies are arranged in elegant boxes, on tiered stands, or as part of a dessert table. Bakers can turn their cookies into visually stunning treats that appeal to the senses and the eyes by adding artistic elements to the presentation.

Accepting the idea of cookie collections or sets enables bakers to use their creations to convey a narrative. Rather than serving individual cookies, a set can tell a story or have a theme. For instance, mittens, snowmen, and snowflakes can be part of a winter wonderland collection, but flip-flops, pineapples, and suns might be part of a tropical paradise set. This method gives the cookie experience a storytelling element and fosters creativity in creating sets that work well together and perfectly embody the occasion.

Cookies become little masterpieces when edible art techniques like fondant decorating, edible painting, and royal icing piping are used to add complexity and depth to them. With its glossy, smooth texture, royal icing is a flexible medium for precise pipe work. The decorator's creativity and talent are the only restrictions on what they can create, ranging from intricate floral arrangements to delicate lace patterns. Fondant has a supple and silky surface ideal for crafting three-dimensional ornaments, enabling the creation of complex embellishments and sculpted forms. Using food-safe paints, edible painting allows designers to express their creativity in a whole new way by allowing them to add subtle shading, delicate details, and customized touches to their cookies.

Textures like lace designs or embossing can enhance the visual appeal of cookies for events that call for sophistication. Rolling out cookie dough can be patterned with embossing rollers or textured mats to create beautiful backgrounds for ornaments. Edible lace or piped royal icing lace patterns provide a delicate, sophisticated touch. These texture-enhanced cookies show off the decorator's talent and add style and visual appeal to a refined dessert table perfect for special occasions.

Cookies are made unforgettable not just by their attractive appearance but also by their careful personalization. Adding names, initials, or critical dates to cookies gives them a personal touch that elevates the celebration. For weddings, baby showers, and milestone birthdays, personalized cookies are delicious presents that give visitors a keepsake they can cherish. Customization goes beyond just writing on cookies; designers can incorporate the recipient's interests, pastimes, or favorite hues to make the sweets incredibly meaningful.

Decorators might investigate options that accommodate different dietary choices and constraints in the spirit of inclusivity. Thanks to the popularity of vegan, gluten-free, and allergy-friendly ingredients, it's now possible to make delectable cookies that satisfy various dietary requirements. This method ensures that everyone enjoys indulging in exquisitely made and unforgettable cookies, irrespective of nutritional limitations. Providing a range of choices—from classic recipes to modified versions—guarantees that everyone may enjoy cookies in an inclusive and accessible manner.

A distinctive and engaging method to make delicacies that will stick in your memory is through cooperative cookie decorating sessions. Whether done with loved ones, close friends, or a group of enthusiasts, decorating cookies together becomes a fun activity that fosters creativity, humor, and the satisfaction of producing something lovely. A cookie decorating soirée for a bridal shower or a holiday cookie exchange are two examples of themed cookie decorating events. Not only is cookie decorating a fun social activity, but it also creates a sense of community as people share design ideas, tips, and tactics.

To sum up, making cookies that will last a lifetime is a beautiful process that blends culinary creativity and the excitement of celebration. Through careful taste selection, exploration of various shapes and themes, and application of artistic skills, bakers can elevate essential cookies into palatable manifestations of happiness and celebration. Their presentation, individuality, and inclusivity make these delights even more memorable, guaranteeing they will become a staple of special events. Since cookies will always have a special place in our hearts and customs, baking excellent cookies will always be a joyous and delectable endeavor to give sweetness to life's most important occasions.

CHAPTER IX

Hosting a Cookie Decorating Party

Planning and Organizing a Festive Cookie Decorating Party

The holidays are a time for happiness, family time, and the fun custom of decorating cookies. Organizing a joyful cookie decorating event is more than simply a cooking project; it's a chance to unite loved ones and friends, encouraging creativity and a sense of community. This essay explores the essential components that lead to a successful and unforgettable event as it dives into organizing and preparing a festive cookie decorating party.

Careful planning is the cornerstone of a successful cookie-decorating party. Start by deciding on the party's goal and theme. Whether the event is a family custom, an informal get-together of friends, or a themed celebration, having a clear vision sets the tone for organizing. To customize the party to the attendees' needs and tastes, consider the participants' age range, the size of the gathering, and any special dietary restrictions.

An essential component of creating excitement and anticipation for the cookie decorating party is sending out invitations. Use your imagination to incorporate the festive theme into the invitations. If you would instead send conventional paper invites with cookie-shaped cutouts, think about sending digital invitations with vibrant and themed themes. Add pertinent information like the date, time, place, and any particular guidelines or themes for decorating the cookies. To improve planning and guarantee that everyone is made to feel welcome, ask attendees to RSVP.

The foundation for a great cookie decorating party is the location. You can organize the celebration at home, rent a community facility, or use ample outdoor space, depending on how many people attend and the atmosphere you want to create. For any baking or food preparation, consider elements like plenty of table space, excellent lighting, and convenient access to kitchen facilities. The idea is to create a welcoming and cozy environment where people feel free to express their ideas.

Naturally, the cookies are the focal point of any cookie decorating party. Decide if you want to bake the cookies ahead of time or if you want to let your guests help. While baking together can provide an engaging and festive touch to the celebration, prebaked cookies save time and allow more attention to be paid to decorating. Ensure you have a range of cookie sizes and shapes to accommodate varying decorating tastes. Offer gluten-free, vegan, or allergy-friendly cookie options if dietary constraints are a factor.

A good cookie decorating party requires a variety of tasty and vibrant icings. Make royal icing in a range of colors, making sure the palette complements the party's theme or the holiday being observed. For vivid and intense colors, use gel food coloring. Provide a variety of piping consistencies, such as flooding and outlining, to accommodate various decorative styles. Provide visitors with couplers, tips, and piping bags so they can accurately express their ideas.

Toppings like sprinkles, edible glitter, colored sugars, and fondant give the cookie-decorating experience the last touches. To avoid spills, arrange these components at conveniently located stations with shakers or little containers. Think about selecting themes that complement the overall style of the party. While whimsical shapes and colors appeal to participants of all ages, edible pearls, metallic dragees, and themed sprinkles can offer a sense of elegance to decorating.

The setting for cookie decorating is essential to the party's success. Ensure that each participant has adequate space at their workstation and that cookies, icing, and decorations are easily accessible. To make cleanup easier, cover tables with disposable tablecloths. Give each guest a separate tray or plate so they may put their cookies together. Provide various decorating tools, including brushes, tiny spatulas, and toothpicks, to suit multiple methods and tastes. Participants may find having a central demonstration station where the host displays decorating tricks and approaches helpful.

Ensure guests have a smooth and delightful experience by breaking down the cookie decorating process into smaller, more manageable parts. First, give a quick introduction and rundown of the stations and equipment for cookie decorating. Consider preparing prebaked cookies for decorating if making is a part of the celebration. Explain how to use royal icing to outline and flood cookies while showcasing various methods and designs. Encourage people to use their imaginations, offering advice and support as required. Provide specific spaces for cookies to dry as the decorating process continues to ensure participants can transport their masterpieces home without smudging.

Add background music to the party's theme to improve the festive vibe. Make a playlist of upbeat, holiday-themed songs to bring even more happiness to the occasion. On the other hand, if room permits, carolers or live music can add to a dynamic and joyous atmosphere. In addition to providing an aural environment, music unifies and improves the experience.

Create a lively and entertaining environment by involving participants in engaging activities beyond cookie decorating. Consider including a cookie exchange so attendees can trade adorned cookies for a fun collection to take home. An enjoyable aspect is added to the party; participants can capture memories with a photo booth with festive props. To add to the fun and excite the celebration, consider holding a cookie decorating competition with minor prizes to encourage friendly rivalry.

Any event would be complete with refreshments, and a cookie decorating party is the same. To go with the cookie theme, think about serving a combination of sweet and savory food. Appetizers, finger foods, and a hot chocolate or beverage station heighten the celebratory mood. Include participants in cookie-related activities, such as a blind taste test or a cookie and beverage pairing, if time permits. When organizing the refreshments, make sure dietary preferences and restrictions are considered.

As the cookie decorating event ends, provide attendees with packaging so they may bring their masterpieces home. The clever addition of cookie boxes, cellophane bags, and festive ribbons enables visitors to share their decorated cookies with friends and family. Think about giving them recipe cards or brief notes thanking them for cooperation. This action provides a personal touch and spreads a joyous mood beyond the occasion.

Cleaning up after a party is essential to ensuring hosts and guests have a good time. Establish dedicated spaces for removing single-use products and assuring recycling containers are easily accessible. Encourage participants to dispose of garbage and return decorating items to their assigned locations to include them in the cleanup process. Making sure the hosting space is left in good shape and prepared for future parties is ensured by a meticulous cleanup.

To sum up, creating a fun cookie decorating party requires careful consideration of every little aspect, planning, and inventiveness. Every event component contributes to its overall success, from the initial plan and invitations to the setup for cookie decorating, interactive activities, and clean up after the party. In addition to producing beautiful memories, a well-planned cookie-decorating party encourages happiness, creativity, and community among attendees. A cookie decorating party becomes a treasured custom that adds cheer and warmth to the holiday season as the delightful smell of freshly made cookies fills the air and laughter reverberates throughout the decorating area.

Invitations, Decorations, and Atmosphere

Beyond simple planning, creating memorable events is an artistic endeavor that involves creating a tapestry of sensations and feelings that guests will carry with them long after the event has ended. Three components—

invitations, decorations, and atmosphere—stand out as the leading designers of a lasting impression in this complex dance of event preparation.

Every event starts with the invitation, a sophisticated messenger that provides essential information about logistics and establishes the overall mood of the gathering. Invitations are the first stroke on the anticipation canvas; they reveal the event's theme, level of formality, and general atmosphere. An exquisitely designed invitation is like the first notes of a symphony—it sets the tone for the event and creates anticipation in guests. It's more than just a sheet of paper or an electronic message; it's a teaser piques interest and anticipation for the event.

The secret to a well-designed invitation is to capture the spirit of the occasion. Whether it's a birthday party, wedding, or corporate event, the invitation acts as a verbal and visual representative, capturing the distinct essence of the occasion. The chosen mood is communicated mainly through typefaces, colors, and graphics. Subdued colors and elegant fonts might be used for a formal event, but bright colors and whimsical visuals might be used for a fun birthday celebration. Essentially, the invitation becomes a sign of things to come, sowing the seeds of expectation that will sprout on the gathering day.

The onus shifts to the decorations after the invitation graciously extends its welcome. These creative components turn a room into a carefully planned area, a sensory-rich setting that ties in with the event's topic. Decorations express a tale without using words; they are the visual poetry of an occasion. Every component adds to the aesthetic narrative, from streamers that emanate celebration to floral arrangements that suggest passion.

Think about a wedding where the right flowers, lighting, and table arrangements can make a room feel like a romantic retreat. The thoughtful placement of centerpieces creates an ambiance that reflects the couple's love story, the gentle glow of the candles, and the subtle interplay of materials. Similarly, a corporate event could use sleek, contemporary décor to project creativity and professionalism. The strategic positioning of logos, material selections, and furniture arrangement all help strengthen the brand identity and foster an environment consistent with the company's values.

When it comes to decorations, the little things are the most important. The little details, like the custom name cards and the well-placed accent lighting, take the design from average to spectacular. Every component is a brushstroke that adds to the event space's beauty. Additionally, decorations are a visual language that tells visitors what feelings to connect with the occasion. A well-decorated space evokes strong feelings in addition to pleasing the eye, providing a holistic experience.

Nevertheless, an event's atmosphere is a symphony of sensory experiences that immerse guests from the moment they walk through the door, unlike decorations, which communicate a visual language. Beyond what is seen, the atmosphere includes everything from the ambient sounds that serve as a background for conversation to the aroma that permeates the space. The intangible quality determines whether guests feel involved, at home, and welcome, and it has the power to make or destroy an event.

For example, music can significantly influence the atmosphere. Songs can create a calming atmosphere, stir excitement in a crowd, or bring back fond memories. From the upbeat beats accompanying a dance floor to the calming melodies following a formal dinner, the music's rhythm and tempo can direct the event's flow. Likewise, lighting is essential for establishing ambiance; warm, low lighting creates a cozy environment, while bright, colorful lighting energizes a room.

Careful attention to detail is applied to all senses to create a memorable atmosphere. The visual feast of a well-curated menu, the soft materials feel, and the delicate cuisine flavor all add to the overall ambiance. To guarantee that visitors are physically comfortable and able to completely immerse themselves in the experience, even the temperature and air quality play minor roles.

An event's atmosphere results from a careful dance between reception and intention. It involves gauging the wants and demands of the guests and designing the space to appeal to them. In an effective event atmosphere, attendees experience themselves as active players in the story instead of passive observers. It's a setting that encourages communication, connection, and, eventually, the creation of enduring memories.

To sum up, the mood, décor, and invitations are the triad that creates the essence of each event. An event's success depends on how well these components work together, starting with the invitation, which makes a story of anticipation, and ending with the décor, which creates a visual and tactile symphony and an immersive atmosphere for guests. Every element adds to the whole experience and creates a lasting impression on the recollections of people participating in the planned festival. In the larger scheme of things, the careful selection of invites, the creative decorating, and the construction of an enthralling ambiance turn a routine get-together into a remarkable, one-of-a-kind event.

Tips for a Successful Cookie Decorating Event

Beyond its origins as a culinary activity, cookie decorating has evolved into a creative and social activity that unites people around the joy of creating tasty works of art. A cookie decorating event depends on careful organization, imagination, and a dash of excitement, whether a more formal affair or a get-together with friends. This essay explores the subtleties that turn an essential cookie into a canvas for culinary expression, delving into the necessary advice for planning a successful cookie decorating event.

Careful planning is the cornerstone of any successful cookie-decorating event. First, choose a location appropriate for the number of attendees and easy mobility. An expansive kitchen, a bright dining area, or even an outside patio might provide the ideal setting for artistic mayhem during cookie decorating. Consider the event's logistics and ensure that everyone has enough space to work and that necessary supplies and materials are easily accessible.

The cookies are crucial because they serve as a blank canvas for inventiveness. Choose a sugar cookie recipe that is adaptable and keeps its shape while baking, making it an excellent base for creative activities. To ensure the icing doesn't accidentally melt during decorating, bake the cookies beforehand and give them enough time to cool. Providing substitute recipes that accommodate different tastes for those with dietary restrictions guarantees inclusivity and expands creative options.

Making a colorful, versatile royal icing is equally essential. Please give them a palette that inspires creativity by dividing the frosting into various colors. Make sure the icing consistency is suitable for flooding and outlining, as this contrast enables fine details and even surfaces. Pre-fill icing bags with multiple tips to suit different decorating styles, such as delicate lines or strong strokes. Having everything close at hand allows participants to focus on the creative process without distraction.

An interactive cookie decorating event depends on people exchanging ideas and techniques with one another. Consider including a brief presentation at the event's start to show off fundamental decorating methods and provide advice on uniformity of icing color and mixing. This inspires seasoned decorators and offers a valuable starting point for novices. To create a collaborative atmosphere that turns the event into a group learning experience, encourage participants to give their advice.

Introduce a theme or a collection of cookie shapes corresponding to the event to strengthen the sense of community. A theme provides an added dimension of fun and coherence to any event, be it a birthday party, holiday get-together, or seasonal celebration. Offering a selection of cookie cutters enables attendees to select forms that speak to them, promoting a wide range of creations that enhance the event's overall visual theme. An aspect of cookie decorating parties that is sometimes disregarded is the significance of appropriate planning and cleanup techniques. Establish a unique location for drying adorned cookies to prevent confusion. To prevent smearing, use parchment paper or drying racks to allow biscuits to set. Also, set up a workspace with paper towels or moist rags for easy cleanup between decorative projects. Participants may concentrate on their artistic activities without being distracted by clutter or the constant need to clean up after themselves when an ordered setting is maintained.

Although decorating cookies is the main focus of a cookie decorating party, you should consider adding other activities to make the event more enjoyable. A beverage bar with hot chocolate, tea, or coffee can go well with a cookie decorating station, creating a warm atmosphere that improves the social side of the event. A cookie exchange or a friendly decorating competition can also add excitement and make the event something to remember while still having a competitive edge.

An essential part of preserving the creativity that emerges throughout the event is photography. Provide a well-lit photo area where participants can display their completed projects. This is a visual souvenir that attendees may treasure and show off, as well as a way to capture the spirit of the occasion. Think of posting pictures from the event on social media sites to build an online showcase that brings the delight of cookie decorating outside the event venue.

Various decorating tools and accessories will accommodate different skill levels while maintaining an inclusive vibe. Providing a wide range of options, from simple piping tips to more complex stencils and edible embellishments, encourages experimentation and pushes individuals' creative limits. Providing reference resources, such as decorating guidelines or tutorials, can be valuable for individuals who need more confidence in their decorating abilities. This can create a supportive environment, allowing everyone to express their artistic flare.

For a cookie decorating event to be successful, timing is essential. Make sure that structured activities and unstructured creativity are balanced. A quick presentation serves as a guide and sets the tone, allowing participants to explore their artistic visions. Instead of using strict timetables that impede the organic flow of creativity, choose an adaptable framework considering the participants' paces and preferences.

To sum up, a good cookie decorating event combines strategic planning, artistic license, and a touch of group spirit harmoniously. Every event component, from the thoughtful choice of location and menu to creating a lively and engaging environment, adds to its overall success. A cookie decorating party becomes an immersive event where creativity reigns supreme when themes are embraced, teamwork is encouraged, and extra activities are included. In addition to enjoying the delectable outcomes, attendees also take home the sweet memories of a genuinely successful cookie decorating event thanks to the shared joy of creating edible works of art.

CHAPTER X

Edible Gifts and Packaging

Turning Your Cookies into Edible Gifts

A sincere, handcrafted present has a timeless appeal in a world overflowing with material goods. Food presents have a unique position among the many alternatives, and baked cookies are one of the best ways to express love and originality. Making homemade cookies into gifts that can be eaten is a way to showcase your culinary prowess and a kind deed that conveys the thought and care that goes into giving. This essay delves into the subtleties of recipe selection, packaging, and the

sentimental value that comes with providing homemade goodies as we examine the art of turning your cookies into delightful edible gifts.

Transforming your cookies into delectable presents starts with choosing the appropriate recipes. Though traditional sugar and chocolate chip cookies are always a hit, consider the recipient's tastes and dietary requirements. Homemade cookies are so versatile that you can experiment with various flavors and textures, such as delicate shortbread and spiced gingerbread. By selecting cookies based on the recipient's preferences, you demonstrate your culinary skills and add a touch of individualization that enhances the experience of giving gifts.

When the cookies are perfectly cooked, the presentation becomes the main attraction. The packaging dramatically influences an appealing visual appeal that heightens the recipient's anticipation. Think about putting the cookies in clear jars or containers that allow the deliciousness to shine through. This gives your homemade treats an artisanal feel that the receiver can appreciate and adds a touch of refinement. Try adding a personalized touch by experimenting with labels, bespoke tags, or elegant ribbons to make the packaging
seem more considerate.

Though aesthetics hold significance, utility must also not be disregarded. Select packaging that keeps the cookies' integrity and freshness intact. Use airtight containers to save cookies from going bad for softer cookies. To prevent breakage, layer more delicate choices, such as sugar cookies with detailed decorations, between sheets of parchment paper. The aim is to provide the recipient with a gastronomic experience that captures the delectability of your dishes in addition to a visual feast.

Considering the recipient's life circumstances adds further thoughtfulness to your gastronomic presence. Are the cookies being given as gifts for a special event like a birthday, celebration, or holiday? Make sure the presentation and packaging complement the event's theme or vibe. Consider using festive holiday decorations and colors that capture the season's essence when selecting a present for someone. This amount of consideration seen in the attention to detail turns the act of giving into a carefully chosen experience that profoundly affects the recipient.

Think of adding a unique touch to the package that conveys a story and its aesthetic appeal. Include a handwritten message or recipe card with your cookies that explains how they were inspired or provides serving ideas. This narrative component gives the gift more depth by establishing a relationship between the donor, the recipient, and the mouthwatering delights inside the package. Sharing the cookies and the tale behind them creates a sense of closeness that turns the gift into a happy moment both parties share.

Variety is the flavor of life—at least when it comes to food presents. Think of assembling a well-chosen cookie collection with various tastes, forms, and textures. This gives the receiver a surprise factor and shows off your versatility as a baker. Every palette can find something they enjoy, from the chewiness of oatmeal cookies to the delicate crumb of almond crescents, thanks to the wide variety available. Every variety of cookies adds to the overall visual appeal of the gift, demonstrating how the art of curation extends to visual presentation.

The cookie canvas is a unique chance for individuals who enjoy artistic expression to display their talent. Try several decorating methods, such as simple chocolate drizzles or elaborate icing designs. Cookies with decorations, particularly those made for a particular theme or event, turn the present from a sugary confection into a tiny artwork. The gift is a monument to artistry and culinary creativity because of the attention to detail, which improves the visual appeal and highlights the care put into each cookie.

Giving delicious presents is a concrete and sensory experience that goes beyond the virtual in the era of digital communication. Presenting a thoughtfully assembled box of cookies expresses time, work, and sincere concern; it differs from the immediate nature of contemporary communication. When you give baked cookies as a present, you give the receiver more than just a tasty treat—you give them a concrete way to express your feelings and a moment of intimacy that happens when they open the package and savor the carefully selected flavors.

Think about how versatile cookies are as presents for events other than special occasions. Making a batch of cookies can be a simple way to say "thinking of you," a sign of support during trying times, or a way to thank a friend for their compassion. Giving culinary presents to others takes on a life of its own, evolving into a wordless dialogue that breaks down barriers and strengthens interpersonal bonds. This exchange elevated cookies from a delicious treat to representing cherished memories and the ties that bind people together.
In summary, transforming your cookies into eatable presents is a complex craft that involves more than just baking. It entails a deliberate choice of recipes, a creative presentation strategy, and a sincere empathy for the feelings that underlie the gift. Giving is transformed into a meaningful experience through the process, with each cookie serving as a messenger of memories and emotions. The art of presenting baked cookies captures the spirit of coziness, inventiveness, and the delight that comes from both giving and receiving, whether for a celebration, a special occasion, or just a plain act of kindness.

Creative Packaging Ideas

Regarding gift-giving, presentation skills are critical in turning a meaningful gesture into an unforgettable occasion. Beyond being aesthetically pleasing, innovative packaging extends the present and gives the receiver additional excitement and expectation. How a gift is wrapped can significantly impact the exchange, whether it is a birthday present, holiday gift, or just a mark of appreciation. This essay delves into imaginative packaging concepts, examining the subtleties of design, materials, and the affective resonance that a visually striking presentation may have on the act of presenting a gift.

The combination of design and utility is the foundation of creative packaging. The wrapping paper selection, which comes in various styles, from classic prints to cutting-edge patterns, acts as the canvas for the innovative project. When choosing wrapping paper, consider the event and the recipient's preferences to create a personalized feeling. Consider using materials other than the typical paper rolls, such as cloth, newspapers, or maps, to give the presentation a distinctive touch. The wrapping paper's texture and design establish the mood visually, luring the receiver to experience the present through their senses even before it is opened.

The last touches to the wrapped canvas are applied with brushstrokes to create ribbons, bows, and embellishments. Try varying the textures and colors to create a cohesive look that goes well with the wrapping paper. A rustic twine provides a little character, yet a traditional satin ribbon may suggest luxury. The arrangement is just as important as the selection of materials; a thoughtfully knotted bow or a cluster of ribbons may take an ordinary offering to a remarkable level. The intention is to arouse awe, turning the unwrapping process into a joyful and anticipatory moment.

Consider including components that engage the recipient in a way that goes beyond the visual for a tactile and engaging experience. Reusable fabric gift wrappers offer an additional touch of thoughtfulness to the gift while also promoting sustainability and environmental friendliness. A multisensory experience is produced by tactile features like textured paper, embossed patterns, or even the insertion of a bit of charm or trinket. Giving a gift also involves touching the recipient, strengthening the bond between the donor and the recipient.

There is more to inventive packaging than just the standard rectangular box. Look into substitute packaging options that capture the spirit of the present while introducing a surprise aspect. Gift-giving containers can be made from mason jars, old tins, or cloth pouches. With its clue of what's within, the container plays a crucial role in the story. This non-traditional method provides a quirky touch and shows that the recipient's preferences and personality were carefully considered. Gift

packaging can be customized in ways other than just the appearance. To add a bit of intimacy, include a handwritten note, a personalized tag, or even a tiny illustration. A personalized note from the giver to the recipient transforms the present from a primary offering to a unique gesture that builds rapport. The message adds a layer of emotional resonance to the whole experience, both as a souvenir and a concrete reminder of the thoughts behind the gift.

The creative packaging procedure might be guided by the occasion's theme or the recipient's hobbies. Whether the presentation is for a birthday, wedding, or holiday, customizing it to fit the occasion makes the whole experience seamless and engaging. For instance, a gift tied with twine and holly can bring up memories of the joyous Christmas season, but wrapping paper and ribbons with a pastel color scheme might be more appropriate for a spring celebration. The present, the packaging, and the occasion are all brought together cohesively by the theme, which serves as a unifying thread.

The craft of innovative packaging might incorporate a handiwork component for those who are daring. Custom graphics, stamped patterns, or even hand-painted wrapping paper lend a unique personal touch to the gift. This interactive method displays inventiveness and demonstrates the amount of work and attention to detail that went into the presentation. The packaging is made with passion, from hand-embossed tags to hand-stitched fabric wrapping, highlighting the significance of the present.

Creative packaging options can be utilized to maximize the gift's size and shape. For more miniature goods, think about using nesting boxes that generate anticipation with each step of the unwrapping process by gradually revealing the layers of the gift. A sequence of nested boxes with tiny surprises inside each brings a playful and exploratory element. Alternatively, consider designing a gift bag with interactive features like pull-out or hidden pockets for more significant things. The unwrapping is transformed into a delightful adventure as the packaging becomes interactive.

The act of physically exchanging gifts has greater relevance in digital communication. The work, consideration, and care put into the act of giving are represented in the creative packaging. It makes the exchange a happy and meaningful event beyond the gift's tangible worth. When a gift is artistically wrapped, it becomes a treasure trove that the recipient is eager to uncover and holds a physical representation of the feelings that went into it.

Creative packaging is not just for individual gifts but also gift-giving occasions. Think about the visual impact of a wedding or birthday party present table that has been beautifully decorated. Incorporating customized touches, a range of package types, and a cohesive theme creates an immersive ambiance that elevates the celebration experience. Giving gifts becomes a shared artistic experience when the presentation is practiced collaboratively.

The creative packaging industry celebrates creativity, inventiveness, and gift-giving joy. It turns giving a gift into a platform for expressing oneself, a way to share feelings, and a way to make enduring memories. Every component of the presentation, including the materials selected, the ribbon arrangements, and the addition of unique accents, adds to its overall effect. When a gift is presented artistically, it transcends from a tangible item to a symbol of the giver's consideration, imagination, and forethought, unwrapping itself a genuine source of joy.

Spreading Joy with Delicious Presents

In a society where good deeds are highly valued, few things have the same profound impact as exchanging delicious gifts. With all the love and care that went into making them, food gifts have a unique power to make people happy and warm. Presenting a wonderful gift, whether a box of baked cookies, a jar of gourmet preserves, or a skillfully constructed cake, transcends the commonplace and fosters moments of shared joy and connection. This essay delves into the art of bringing joy through delectable gifts, examining the value of food gifts, carefully selecting candies, and how these gestures affect the giver and the recipient.

Food's fundamental universality lies at the core of the happiness experienced from culinary gifts. Food is a language that connects people and evokes memories across linguistic and cultural divides. Giving food as a gift is not only about giving something to eat; it's also about offering something of oneself. A recipe handed down through the years, a dish sparked by a treasured memory, or a creation resulting from culinary experimentation—whatever the source, the present becomes a material manifestation of the giver's identity, providing a taste of their narrative.

Choosing the ideal treat for a gourmet gift is a skill in and of itself. It entails carefully considering the recipient's dietary needs, preferences, and tastes. A thoughtfully selected present indicates a level of consideration that extends beyond giving; it means a sincere knowledge of the recipient's preferences. Please consider the occasion as well; whether it's a birthday, a holiday, or a way to show someone you appreciate them, customizing the culinary gift to fit the occasion adds a special touch.

Cooks are the perfect representation of culinary happiness. These baked treats, which range from traditional chocolate chips to elaborately decorated sugar cookies, provide an outlet for artistic expression and a vehicle for sentimentality. A thoughtfully prepared and beautifully presented basket of handmade cookies may make someone's day. Just the smell of freshly baked cookies can arouse sentiments of coziness and nostalgia, enhancing the delight of the culinary presence through a multisensory experience.

Carefully and precisely made preserves and jams provide a taste of seasonal abundance. These culinary gifts capture the season's spirit and the ingredients' flavors, such as a spiced apple preserve that embodies fall or a jar of strawberry jam from luscious summer berries. Homemade preserves are a delicious delicacy and a sensory feast due to their bold, rich colors and inviting scents.

Cakes are a symbol of celebration and are often associated with special occasions. A well-crafted and exquisitely adorned cake can be the focal point for a milestone, anniversary, or birthday celebration. Giving a cake as a present signifies more than just edible delight; it's a way to express gratitude and send well wishes for happiness and prosperity. Whether it is a simple vanilla sponge or a complex fondant design, the cake represents joy shared by all.

Regarding culinary presents, the packaging is just as important as the food. The presentation of a basic jar of preserves or a box of cookies is elevated by imaginative and intelligent packaging, creating a visually appealing treat. Think of utilizing clear jars that highlight the vivid hues of jams or going with ornamental boxes that give the cookies a hint of refinement. The packaging sets the scene for the delicious surprise to be revealed, acting as a prelude to the excitement.

Giving a gourmet gift is more than just material things; it's a time of bonding and celebration. The transaction becomes a ritual, a ceremonial offering that transcends economic exchange. These moments become cherished memories, whether the thrill of giving someone a beautifully wrapped package or the suspense of seeing a loved one open a gourmet surprise. The shared experiences of enjoying the delicacies and the conversations over a cake or a cup of tea deepen the act of giving and creating a sense of community.

Food gifts are not just for formal events; they may be potent ways to show support and affection in trying times. A pot of soup, a tray of warm baked goods, or a prepared dinner can bring comfort and nourishment during difficult times. Giving someone a hearty and comforting meal expresses sympathy and a desire to provide real help and consolation.

Food gifts bring happiness that lasts longer than the moment they are given. It sticks in the mind and leaves a deep impression on the recipient's heart. The gift takes on symbolic meaning in the connection between the giver and the recipient, representing moments of joy, laughing, and everyday bliss. This is how culinary gifts have the fantastic power to stand the test of time and become treasured recollections that bring a smile to one's face.

The effects of delivering delectable gifts reach both the giver and the recipient. Making culinary presents becomes a labor of love and a way to show care and ingenuity. Measuring ingredients, stirring batter, and meticulously packaging the goodies takes time, but the process is contemplative and rewarding. It's a self-care gesture, a conscious moment that enables the giver to integrate their positive energy into the food.

The satisfaction that comes from sharing delectable gifts is what makes them so enjoyable. A feeling of warmth and contentment fills the giver when they see the recipient's expression of joy and gratitude. Giving becomes a joyful personal endeavor, strengthening the vital link between giving and contentment. Regarding culinary gifts, the donor and the recipient share a mutually enjoyable experience that intensifies the good feelings connected to giving.

To sum up, the craft of distributing happiness through delectable gifts honors relationships, ingenuity, and quality time spent together. Culinary gifts are the epitome of care and consideration, whether cakes, cookies, preserves, or other goodies. Giving becomes more than just the material components of the gift; it's a deed that builds relationships, makes memories, and brings happiness in both anticipated and unforeseen circumstances. Food is a language that allows us to express both flavors and feelings, creating enduring relationships and bringing the richness of joyous occasions into our shared lives.

CONCLUSION

Readers have been taken on a lovely voyage through the pages of "Festive Shapes and Sugar Sprinkles Unleashed: Cookie Decorating Extravaganza," where they are transported into a world where edible artistry is created with sugar and imagination has no bounds. With its colorful cover, the e-book entices readers with an extravagant experience while introducing inexperienced and experienced bakers to the fascinating world of cookie decorating. The e-book has revealed the techniques for turning primary forms into edible works of beauty, promoting cookie decorating to the level of an art form, perfect for both festive occasions and ordinary treats.

Readers were taken on a gastronomic journey that goes beyond the norm as they went through the complexities of selecting the ideal forms, investigating cutting-edge methods, and realizing the wonder of sugar sprinkles. The e-book's subtitle perfectly captures its core message: it's not simply about decorating cookies— instead, it's about letting readers express themselves through the delicious canvases that are cookies. The e-book successfully demystified cookie decorating so anyone could learn how to do it. The e-book offers a thorough guide for everyone interested in baking at home, whether they are an enthusiastic baker wishing to improve their techniques or someone searching for ideas for a particular event. The thoughtful balancing act between artistic encouragement and technical advice guarantees that readers will discover delight and self-expression while learning the nuances of the craft.

The e-book encourages a spirit of festivity and celebration in addition to its practical components of cookie decorating. Every page flip exposes the possibility of transforming routine cookies into spectacular delights and moments into memories. The e-book's subtitle, "Cookie Decorating Extravaganza," aptly describes the joy and profusion of inventiveness it inspires.

Finally, "Festive Shapes and Sugar Sprinkles Unleashed: Cookie Decorating Extravaganza" is more than simply a cookbook; it's a call to adventure where sugar turns into a medium for creative edible art and cookies become lovely manifestations of creative imagination. Readers will leave this e-book inspired to add a dash of creativity and a touch of sweetness to any event, in addition to the technical know-how of cookie decorating. It's an occasion to honor the delight that arises from crafting delectable works of art and savoring them with those you care about, transforming every moment into a festivity of tastes and forms.

Thank you for buying and reading/ listening to our book. If you found this book useful/ helpful please take a few minutes and leave a review on the platform where you purchased our book. Your feedback matters greatly to us.

9 798869 133571